Praise for *Becoming Whole:*
Isn't the Am

MW01038837

There is no one from whom I've learned ↳
poverty relief than Brian Fikkert. I am excited to see him team up with Kelly Kapic in what amounts to a "taking the gloves off" explanation of the only answer for human corruption. Fikkert and Kapic show that because life consists of so much more than money, it takes more than money to address poverty and its underlying causes. This book is an essential component in the library of any Christian interested in promoting healthy, sustainable, poverty-relief and human advancement.

J. D. GREEAR | 62nd President, The Southern Baptist Convention; author of *Not God Enough: Why Your Small God Leads to Big Problems*; Pastor, The Summit Church, Raleigh-Durham, NC

Jesus announced, from the very onset of His ministry, His love for the poor (Luke 4:18). Some spiritualize away this concern for the poor, the way others try to spiritualize away His miracles. Others seek to alleviate poverty in fragmented, counterproductive ways. In this fascinating new book, Brian Fikkert and Kelly Kapic call Christians to where Jesus is already: in the fight for whole persons, body and soul. This book will not just awaken you to the plight of global poverty, but will also give you hope as we seek to follow Jesus together for the sake of the poor of the world.

RUSSELL MOORE | President, The Ethics & Religious Liberty Commission of the Southern Baptist Convention

Here's a Christian book about poverty like no other. It offers both a prophetic critique of Western culture and a gospel-centered challenge to the church. This book inspires think bigger and more biblically about our approach to mission in general and development in particular. A must read.

KRISH KANDIAH | Founding Director, Home for Good and author of *God is Stranger: Finding God in Unexpected Places*

In *Becoming Whole*, Fikkert and Kapic build upon the watershed legacy of *When Helping Hurts* by challenging latent assumptions and awakening essential truth. Becoming Whole is a torch of wisdom to lift high, a beacon to help us to exemplify God's love in cultures across the world and also our own backyards. Read at your own risk, however: these words will transform!

STEPHAN BAUMAN | Coauthor of *Seeking Refuge*
Former president and CEO of World Relief

This is a book about transformation. I'm grateful that it's not just about how American Christians can help transform the poor, although that is a worthy topic. No, as surrendered people, we need to constantly yield to the Holy Spirit for our own transformation—to become more and more like Jesus Christ. And we are not truly whole until we give and serve and love like Jesus. There is no more urgent, inspiring, and satisfying mission than bringing God's vision of fullness of life to the ends of the earth. Thank you, Brian Fikkert and Kelly Kapic, for this helpful resource for our journey!

EDGAR SANDOVAL SR. | President, World Vision U.S.

Those of us who have tasted the American Dream know that it's not all it's cracked up to be. And when you understand what's happening in the rest of the world, you realize that pursuing it keeps you on the sidelines of God's great mission. You miss the most exciting adventure there is in life: demonstrating the love of Christ to the "least of these" in ways that draw people to the cross of Christ. *Becoming Whole* is a remarkable sequel to *When Helping Hurts*, and it should be required reading for ministry workers, church leaders, donors, laypeople—everyone responding to God's call to change the world.

RICHARD STEARNS | President Emeritus, World Vision U.S., and author of *The Hole in Our Gospel* and *Unfinished*

Thanks to the principles of love and leadership as articulated in this book, as well as in the related work, *When Helping Hurts*, the church I serve has been able to come alongside disadvantaged, vulnerable, oppressed, and marginalized communities in more informed, life-giving, and sustainable ways. Backed with sound biblical theology and practical guidance and stories, *Becoming Whole* is a must for any Christian community aiming to make a difference. I can't recommend this book highly enough.

SCOTT SAULS | Senior pastor of Christ Presbyterian Church in Nashville, Tennessee Author of *Befriend* and *Irresistible Faith*

The big story (or the metanarrative) that one lives by is not benign; rather, it really, really matters. Our brothers, Fikkert and Kapic, show us how to identify and jettison false metanarratives, like the American Dream, expressive individualism, and consumerism so that we can wisely appropriate and live by the True Big Story found in Scripture for the sake of escorting the poor from their impoverishment to a flourishing position, for the sake of our flourishing and personal wholeness, and for the sake of the flourishing of our communities and cities.

LUKE BOBO | Director of Curriculum and Resources, Made to Flourish

The kingdom of God is about life as God intends. In *Becoming Whole*, Brian Fikkert and Kelly Kapic help us understand the robust narrative that the kingdom creates and supports. Unfortunately, we have settled for puny competing storylines that make people poor—in every way. The Spirit is shouting to the Western church to abandon the worldviews and idols that are keeping us from becoming whole. This book serves as a gracious but prophetic invitation to partner with God in his mission to enable us to become fully human.

REGGIE MCNEAL | Author of *Kingdom Come* and *Kingdom Collaborators*

Becoming Whole is about the rest of the story, our story and how having it right can help in dealing with poverty and the real needs of people. It examines cultures and religions, even religions that claim they have nothing to do with religion. It is revealing and will cause people to reflect in fresh ways on how they see the world and our role in it.

DARRELL L. BOCK | Executive Director for Cultural Engagement, Howard G. Hendricks Center for Christian Leadership and Cultural Engagement; Senior Research Professor of New Testament Studies, Dallas Theological Seminary

Becoming Whole is a hard-hitting, transparent read that will force you to think and act differently as you are confronted with poverty at home and abroad. It will help you understand the root of poverty, whether the unhappiness of the affluent West or the material poverty in the global South. This book will introduce you to an alternative universe, one in which human flourishing, born inside of man through a change in the heart and mind, bears external fruit in the present reality of the coming of the City of God. Metaphysical capital is more important than physical capital in the path to human flourishing.

DARROW MILLER | Author of *Discipling Nations*
Cofounder of Disciple Nations Alliance

Becoming Whole challenges the basis for our best intentions toward the poor, which are often consciously or subconsciously founded on American materialism rather than a holistic Christian view of transformation. Although it is a fitting prequel and sequel to *When Helping Hurts*, it is more than this. It lays an engaging yet theologically comprehensive guide to the foundations of human flourishing.

BRUCE WYDICK | Professor of Economics, University of San Francisco
Distinguished Research Affiliate, University of Notre Dame

Praise for *A Field Guide to Becoming Whole: Principles for Poverty Alleviation Ministry*

I've been waiting for a field guide like this, which provides formative stories and tangible best practices to help address brokenness and poverty through the pursuit of personal, communal, and systemic transformation. The biblical concept of becoming whole and intertwined peace is not just a response to these systemic issues but God's intended hope and call for humanity.

MARY GLENN | Urban Studies Affiliate Professor, Fuller Seminary School of Intercultural Studies (and Chaplain for the Los Angeles County District Attorney's Office)

This is one of the most pragmatic and Christ-centered books for anyone engaged in the work to alleviate poverty. Fikkert and Kapic offer a systematic and comprehensive approach based on many years of experience on what to do, and especially what not to do. They identify key practices and offer Ministry Design Principles that will liberate both the helpers and the so-called helped in order to apply God's story in our various ministries.

ALEXANDER JUN | Professor of Higher Education at Azusa Pacific University

With honesty and humility, *A Field Guide to Becoming Whole* roots out the invisible idol of the American Dream that has seduced many Western Christians and tragically hampered efforts at poverty alleviation. Fikkert and Kapic offer pointed and practical advice, reminding us that God's kingdom is an upside-down world where the pursuit of wholeness—rather than wealth—honors the inherent dignity and worth of all stakeholders.

ELISSA YUKIKO WEICHBRODT | Associate professor of art at Covenant College

I've been waiting for a follow-up to *When Helping Hurts* that would give sound, biblical, practical, and replicable counsel to those trying to help marginalized people in our communities. *Becoming Whole* and *A Field Guide to Becoming Whole* do not disappoint! Here we have tools that can be used with leaders at every level in the church so that we can do good works that protect dignity, foster productivity, and attend to systemic and spiritual forces that limit human flourishing. Read this and be repaid with wisdom for the work of ministry!

THABITI ANYABWILE | Pastor of Anacostia River Church (Washington, DC)

I used to hear this cliché in Christian circles, "Those who are heavenly minded are no earthly good." However, the truth is that heavenly mindedness leads to the most earthly good. That is, those who grasp "God's goals for human beings and His way of achieving those goals" are positioned on the foundation that will not give way as we strive through the ups and downs of trying to love our materially poor neighbors well. Yet, we still want to know what to do in practice. If that describes you, your church, or your ministry, this is your book. The best theology applies the Word of God to the practical areas of life. Kelly Kapic and Brian Fikkert have done just that in *A Field Guide to Becoming Whole*. Chock-full of real-life stories, Scripture, biblical principles, pointed questions and considerations, they have done an invaluable service for those who want to see all of God's image bearers flourish.

IRWYN INCE | Pastor at Grace DC Presbyterian Church and Executive Director of the Grace DC Institute for Cross-Cultural Mission

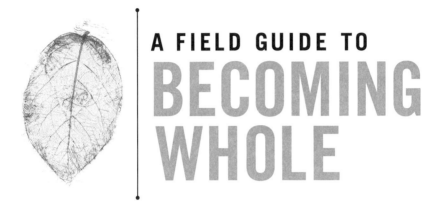

A FIELD GUIDE TO
BECOMING WHOLE

Principles for Poverty Alleviation Ministries

BRIAN FIKKERT
& KELLY M. KAPIC

MOODY PUBLISHERS
CHICAGO

Published in association with the literary agency of Wolgemuth & Associates.

Edited by Kevin P. Emmert
Interior design: Erik M. Peterson
Cover design: Stephen Vosloo
Cover photo of leather notebook copyright © 2019 by kitthanes / Adobe Stock (127534445). All rights reserved.
Cover photo of leaf courtesy of Laura Haley.
Author photo for Brian Fikkert and Kelly Kapic: Tad Evearitt, Covenant College

ISBN: 978-0-8024-1946-0

We hope you enjoy this book from Moody Publishers. Our goal is to provide high-quality, thought-provoking books and products that connect truth to your real needs and challenges. For more information on other books and products written and produced from a biblical perspective, go to www.moodypublishers.com or write to:

Moody Publishers
820 N. LaSalle Boulevard
Chicago, IL 60610

1 3 5 7 9 10 8 6 4 2

Printed in the United States of America

To Henry and Doris Fikkert.
Words cannot express my gratitude for
parents who taught and lived out the good news
of the kingdom of God.
~ Brian

To Gary and Linda Kapic.
I'm so grateful for parents who taught me
how much love, community, and service matter.
~ Kelly

CONTENTS

FOREWORD

One of my more embarrassing travel mistakes happened about fifteen years ago when I carefully, safely, and efficiently drove to Washington, DC's Dulles airport to catch a flight for a speaking engagement. I made good time without getting a speeding ticket or putting anyone at risk. I think I even managed to pray for the sick and grieving during my journey.

The problem was that my flight was actually leaving from Washington, DC's Reagan airport, about twenty-five miles away.

The process of getting to my destination was executed quite well; it's just that the destination itself was wrong. I'm sorry to say that I was not engaged in intercession for the sick and grieving as I drove frantically to Reagan airport. What speech occurred inside my car during that drive more likely led to the Lord's grieving.

If your destination is wrong, it doesn't matter how well you get there—how intentional, thoughtful, or caring you are in getting there. You still end up in the wrong place.

This *Field Guide* offers a road map for getting to the destination we ought to be aiming for when we (as individuals, congregations, and nonprofit ministries) are seeking to love our materially poor neighbors. It is bulging with insightful and practical principles for the journey, but its greatest contribution is its clarity on the destination.

That clarity emerges from three sources: careful attention to biblical anthropology, years of work in economically distressed communities at home and abroad, and a clear-eyed critique of contemporary American culture.

The first helps us understand far better what we human beings are made for (as well as what we are made of). The second produces a set of tested-in-real-life recommendations that are both practical and pointed in the right direction. The third strips away a great deal of mostly unnoticed clutter in our thinking and assumptions that dangerously hinders truly effective—and, more importantly, faithful—work. Taken together, they lead to a destination for both ministry leaders and materially poor people that aligns with our very good God's very good intentions for us.

Those good intentions, this *Field Guide* makes clear, do not equate to the definition of human flourishing provided by the narrative of the American consumerism.

And that's the nub. The painful truth is that despite the Bible verses that may adorn our letterhead and the prayers with which we begin our programs, at least some of what actually happens in Christian ministry to the poor is pointed in the wrong direction. We non-poor Christians have a destination in view that in practice may amount to middle-class suburbia with some Jesus added in. Certainly, we are interested in saving souls. And rightly we seek to ease the financial stresses—and all their attendant woes—that we witness. But to the extent that we ourselves have become satisfied with what passes for "normal" middle-class life in highly individualistic, dangerously materialistic America, we may unwittingly guide our neighbors to a destination far from God's desired finale. Because God wants far more for the poor than a materialistic, hyperindividualistic version of the American Dream plus Jesus. God wants us all restored to our vocation as priest-kings joining our King Jesus in the mission of renewing all things. He desires nothing less for us than the recovery of all that was lost in the Fall: the shalom of peace with God, with self, with others, and with creation. He wants us to truly flourish—with sufficiency of economic provision to be sure, but also with an abundance of meaning, love, purpose, community, laughter, resiliency, and self-giving.

As many readers will be aware, this book follows the publication of *When Helping Hurts: How to Alleviate Poverty Without Hurting the*

Poor. . . and Yourself. God has used that volume to shift the thinking of literally thousands of Christ followers and it has done more than any other work I know of to improve Christian engagement with the poor. This *Field Guide*, though, goes even deeper and further. Its twenty principles for ministry paint a beautiful picture of what "helping that helps" looks like.

There's no good prescription in the absence of good diagnosis; without an accurate understanding of the causes of persistent poverty, our efforts to alleviate it are doomed to fail. Some readers will be surprised by the list of five key factors that Fikkert and Kapic cite, but I hope none will quit reading too soon. These authors take seriously the natural and supernatural realities bearing on the misery in our world—*just like the Bible does.* They actually believe that God's Word has the best, most reliable guidance to offer for the fight against poverty. If your ministry is genuinely committed to grounding your work in the Scriptures, then this is the book for you. But be prepared to be reminded that this work of transformation is really far more about what *God* can (and does) do than about what you and your ministry does. I suspect that you will be humbled by this book. I know I was. You will be challenged to pray far more, acting on a daily basis as though God really is present and active. You will be encouraged to do two things that may feel rather unfamiliar: (1) to share power, inviting those you came to serve into the design of your programs, and (2) to encourage the poor to give sacrificially, understanding that such self-giving is a vital part of genuine human flourishing.

This is a book for ministry leaders about doing better ministry. The principles here offer a kind of matrix against which to assess current work, and to make changes that will better align that work with the good news of the kingdom. To the extent these recommendations are implemented, I believe ministries will see heartening transformation in the lives of those they are seeking to serve. This is a book, in short, that will help us help the poor.

But it's not only about changing the poor. It's equally about changing *us*, the non-materially-poor. So be prepared not only for some best practices for what you can do for them. In this journey toward true flourishing, God wants to grow you (and me) as well as the poor. For, you see, it's not that we have arrived and now are showing them the way. Rather, we're on the journey together, with God in the driver's seat.

And thankfully, He knows exactly where to take us.

AMY L. SHERMAN
Senior Fellow at the Sagamore Institute and author of *Kingdom Calling: Vocational Stewardship for the Common Good*

PREFACE

In 2009, Steve Corbett and I (Brian) wrote *When Helping Hurts: How to Alleviate Poverty without Hurting the Poor . . . and Yourself* (WHH), wherein we articulated a biblically based, relationally focused approach to caring for people who are poor. We argued that while we should do more to help materially poor people, good intentions are not enough. It is possible to hurt poor people in the process of trying to help them. So, we need to abandon strategies that undermine dignity, diminish capacity, and create unhealthy dependency. And we need to increase the use of approaches that are truly empowering.

In the ten years since *WHH* was published, we have received many questions about what to do in a wide range of situations. The causes of poverty are extremely complex and each situation is somewhat unique, so there is no way to answer all these questions. However, it is possible to articulate a systematic model and a series of principles that can guide readers as they seek to be faithful in their various settings. *Becoming Whole: Why the Opposite of Poverty Isn't the American Dream*, the foundation for the book you now hold in your hands, provides such a model, explaining the biblical story of change: God's goals for human beings and His way of achieving those goals. Building on that foundation, this *Field Guide* articulates twenty "Ministry Design Principles" (organized in six categories to help us remember them) that can be used to inform any poverty alleviation ministry.

HOW DO THESE BOOKS RELATE TO *WHEN HELPING HURTS*?

Becoming Whole provides a more systematic treatment of the underlying concepts and principles foundational to *WHH*. As such, it is sort of a prequel to *WHH*, and readers of both books will definitely notice some overlap.

At the same time, a large amount of material in *Becoming Whole* is not in *WHH*. In particular, drawing on recent insights from theologians, philosophers, scientists, and practitioners, *Becoming Whole* employs deeper theology, anthropology, and cosmology than *WHH* in order to articulate a model of human and cultural change that can be used to improve any poverty alleviation initiative. Building upon that foundation, this *Field Guide* then articulates principles that can be implemented to design more effective poverty alleviation ministries. Some of these principles are in *WHH*, but many of them are not. Hence, because so much of the material is new, in some sense these two books are the sequel to *WHH*.

So should you read *WHH* or this series first? It's up to you! However, we guess that most people would benefit from reading *WHH* first, then reading *Becoming Whole*, and then reading this *Field Guide*. The reason for this is that some of the concepts in these two books are more challenging to grasp than those in *WHH*, making this series a somewhat more advanced treatment of effective poverty alleviation. It is essential to read *Becoming Whole* before reading this *Field Guide*, as this *Field Guide* assumes readers are familiar with the concepts and terms described in *Becoming Whole*. If you need a quick refresher, Appendix C contains a brief overview of its main themes. As we present the Ministry Design Principles here, we frequently remind readers of some of the key ideas in *Becoming Whole*, showing how these principles connect to the foundational ideas set forth in *Becoming Whole*.

INTENDED AUDIENCE

Like *Becoming Whole*, this book is relevant for anybody seeking to alleviate poverty, including ministry leaders, staff, volunteers, boards, donors, and others. It is particularly focused on those involved with Christian ministries that are directly interfacing with materially poor people. Hence, some of the content will be slightly less relevant for organizations working in other domains—like organizations seeking to change public policy at a national or international level. However, even readers working in such arenas should find most of the content to be highly relevant to their work.

GETTING OUR STORY STRAIGHT

At the heart of poverty alleviation is change. We are trying to help poor people move from their current condition to a better one. Fostering such change requires us to understand the very nature of human beings, of human flourishing, and of God Himself. God has a plan for changing the entire world—including poor people and ourselves—and since God is all-powerful, we would be wise to get on board with His story, His plan for change.

These issues are deeply theological in nature. As a result, I asked my dear friend Kelly M. Kapic to join me as a coauthor on the two books in this series. Kelly is far too humble to say this about himself, but he is an internationally respected theologian who has focused much of his work on the Trinity and on exploring questions about human nature and relationships, making him an ideal partner for this project. Just as Steve Corbett has been a huge mentor to me in general and in the writing of *WHH* in particular, Kelly has been discipling me on these theological issues for the past decade, deeply impacting me both professionally and personally. Although there are two authors, whenever "I" appears in this book, it refers to me (Brian).

THE HEROES ON THE FRONT LINES

We would like to highlight two challenges in writing a book about subjects like poverty alleviation and the gospel.

First, our culture often gives lots of accolades to authors. But the real heroes are the sacrificial servants working in front line ministry, who normally don't have time to write books. Although our work with the Chalmers Center for Economic Development at Covenant College gives us years of experience in the field of poverty alleviation, it is the faithful practitioners who are the real heroes, as they seek to hold together ministry that is holistic amid the endless storms of life. This book is meant to honor these faithful servants, highlighting the many lessons we have learned from them about both working in poverty alleviation and living faithfully in this broken world. We want theology, research, and practice to be held together, rather than pitted against one another. We want compassion and confession, mercy and meaning, realism and hope. We don't want to choose. So, inspired by many on the front lines, we are offering you what we pray will be biblically, academically, and experientially sound guidance that will help all of us in our diverse callings to see the embodiment of the gospel in our lives and communities.

Second, we authors are very much a work in progress. As our families, friends, and coworkers can attest, we are a long, long way from becoming whole. We struggle every day to live out the concepts in these books, and often we fail more than we succeed. That said, we have confidence "that he who began a good work in us will carry it on to completion until the day of Christ Jesus" (Phil. 1:6), that great day when we'll join all God's people in finally becoming whole (Phil. 1:6). Come quickly, Lord Jesus!

HOW TO USE THIS BOOK

We hope God uses this *Field Guide* to affect your mind, feelings, and actions. Such impact is less likely to happen if you simply read through the book. Toward that end, there are "Questions for Reflection" after each Ministry Design Principle. It is vital that you take the time to prayerfully and thoughtfully work through these questions, as they are an integral part of engaging with the material and applying it to your own life and ministry.

HOW *NOT* TO USE THESE BOOKS

We hope *Becoming Whole* and this *Field Guide* will enable readers to foster more effective approaches to poverty alleviation. One of the keys to making this happen will be for donors to increase funding for more effective ministries and to decrease funding for those that are less effective. However, in most cases, these books should *not* be used as the basis for immediately cutting off funding to a ministry. No ministry is perfect, including the Chalmers Center, under whose auspices this book has been written. Moreover, some of the concepts that will be discussed are new ideas to many ministries. They need to be given time to process these concepts and to determine whether they need to make any adjustments to their work. An attitude of patience and grace should prevail, since all of us—ministries, donors, and materially poor people—are still in process this side of Christ's second coming.

That said, we wholeheartedly believe the concepts and principles discussed in these books are profoundly important, and that widespread disregard of these ideas can do real harm to materially poor people and to those who are trying to help them. Thus, in cases in which a ministry is clearly doing considerable harm and is unwilling to even consider making changes, it may be necessary to remove funding from this ministry relatively quickly.

May God grant all of us the wisdom and humility we need to truly help without hurting.

ABOUT THE ANECDOTES

To the best of our knowledge, all the anecdotes included in this book are true, with the exception of Absco's story in chapter 1, which is a composite of stories that are quite common in the Majority World. However, the names and details of some individuals, churches, and organizations have been changed to protect their identities, unless those names have been previously revealed in other publications from which the anecdotes were taken.

ADDITIONAL RESOURCES

These two books are only an introduction to some incredibly complex issues. You will find additional resources and learning opportunities at www.becomingwholebook.com and through the Chalmers Center (www.chalmers.org).

WE NEED GOD'S HELP

We do not want this *Field Guide* to be simply an intellectual exercise. Rather, we pray that God will use this book, as imperfect as it is, to deeply impact the lives of His people. Toward that end, let us join with Phillis Wheatley, a West African girl sold into slavery in Boston in 1761, who prayed:

> O Lord my God! instruct my ignorance
> & enlighten my Darkness
> Thou art my King, take [thou]
> The entire possession of [all] my
> powers & faculties & let me be
> no longer under the dominion
> of sin.[1]

CHAPTER ONE

IMPROVING THE ONLY TRUE STORY

Tell someone to do something, and you change their life—for a day; tell someone a story and you change their life.[1]

—N. T. WRIGHT, THEOLOGIAN, 1992

Every community needs a big story, a story that frames our lives and our understanding of the world. . . . Therefore, before we set out to accompany the transformation of others, we need to be sure we are clear on the biblical story that has the final say on our individual stories.[2]

—BRYANT MYERS, DEVELOPMENT EXPERT, 2011

Absco has had enough. For generations, his ancestors have scraped and clawed, begging the soil in rural Kenya to yield a harvest. When the weather is good, life is bearable. But when the rains don't come—he shudders to even think about it. Absco has already lost one child, her malnourished body too weak to fight off the malaria. Enough is enough. It's time for a change.[3]

But change is largely a foreign concept in Absco's village. Life there is about loyalty—to the ancestral spirits, to the tribe, to the family, and to the land. So when Absco announces that he will migrate to the city to seek a better life, he is viewed as an arrogant traitor. "Do you think you are better than the rest of us? What about your responsibilities here?" The questions hurt, and Absco is torn, but he's determined that no more of his children will die.

So off he goes to the city, leaving his wife and kids back in the village until he can get established. Unfortunately, things don't go as well there as Absco had hoped. Day after day, he knocks on doors looking for work, but there are far more job seekers than jobs available. With little education and no connections, Absco is unable to find work that pays enough to support his family. Lonely and discouraged, he longs to return home, but how can he face his family and village? In addition to being an arrogant traitor, he is now a failure as well.

Each night, Absco joins thousands of others like him in a slum on the edge of the city. Exhausted from another day of looking for work, he collapses on the dirt floor of the shack that he's made from scraps of wood. There, he sleeps until the sun comes up, signaling the start of another day of fruitless job searching.

One night, Absco is particularly lonely and depressed. Seeking to deaden the pain, he ventures out of his shack to try the local brew concocted by some other slum dwellers. With his inhibitions lowered, Absco then succumbs to the invitation from one of the prostitutes loitering on the corner.

Three months later, a clinic gives Absco the bad news: he has HIV.

THE SHAPING POWER OF STORIES OF CHANGE

Imagine you want to design a ministry to help the many people like Absco in this Kenyan slum. You will need to answer many questions:

- **What type of assistance will be provided?** A feeding program? Job training? Health care? Improved farming techniques in the village? Evangelism? Biblical discipleship?

- **Who will provide the assistance?** A local church? An existing parachurch ministry in Kenya? A government agency? A new organization you will start?

- **How will the assistance be delivered?** One on one? Group setting? Radio? Smartphones?

- **Who will pay for the assistance?** Western donors? Kenyan donors? Program participants?

- **What will be the metrics for success?** Greater consumption? Improved health? Strengthened families? Less migration? Spiritual growth?

- **Who will decide the answers to all these questions?** You? Donors? Local churches? Program participants?

A poverty alleviation ministry is fundamentally about promoting change. It's about helping poor people and communities move to a better situation than their present one. So, effective poverty alleviation requires us to know where we are trying to go and how we can get there. In other words, we need a sound "story of change" or, as it is often referred to in the social services sector, a sound "theory of change." At its core, a story of change is your ministry's answer to two fundamental questions:

1. What is the goal of life?
2. How can that goal be achieved?

Take a moment and reflect on these two questions. It is possible that you've never consciously answered these questions before, but you have answers to them nonetheless. Most of us have unknowingly internalized our surrounding culture's story of change, conditioning us to *automatically* and *subconsciously* think, feel, and act the ways that we do as a matter of *habit*.[4] Consequently, even though it's often unarticulated, our story of change dramatically impacts every aspect of our lives, including the way we design our poverty alleviation ministries. *If we want to help without hurting, we've got to get our story straight.*

COMPETING STORIES OF CHANGE

Our story of change reflects our "metanarrative"—our understanding of the nature of God, of human beings, and of how the world works.

As we discussed in *Becoming Whole* chapter 2, some scholars argue that there are three foundational religious perspectives in the world: *traditional religion, Western Naturalism, and historic Christianity*, the other religious perspectives being blends of these three (Figure 1.1).[5]

FIGURE 1.1

Three-Part Model of World Religious Perspectives

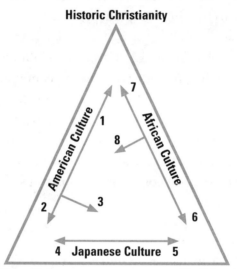

1) American Christians; 2) American Secularists; 3) New Agers in North America;
4) Western-influenced Japanese; 5) Shintoists; 6) African Traditional Religionists;
7) African Christians; 8) Secular influences radiating out of Christianity.

Adapted from Gailyn Van Rheenen, "Animism, Secularism, and Theism: Developing a Tripartite Model for Understanding World Cultures," *International Journal of Frontier Missions* 10, no. 4 (October 1993): 171.

Traditional religion, which is common among poor people in the Majority World (Africa, Asia, and Latin America), believes that the material world is controlled by spiritual forces. In this perspective, human beings are not really in charge of developing creation; rather, life is about hunkering down to avoid disharmony with one's family, tribe, nature, and the spirits.

Western Naturalism, which has had a tremendous influence on Western civilization, believes the world is fundamentally material in nature. Consistent with this, it views human beings as highly individualistic, materialistic creatures that derive happiness from obtaining greater and greater material consumption—the American Dream is the story of change, which we discussed in *Becoming Whole* chapter 3.

In chapter 4 of *Becoming Whole*, we showed that the Western church has largely mixed Western Naturalism with historic Christianity to create Evangelical Gnosticism, a metanarrative that separates the spiritual and material realms (point 1 in Figure 1.1). This has produced a story of change in which the goal is to get one's soul to heaven for eternity and, as in the case of Western Naturalism, live the American Dream now.

When Westerners attempt to alleviate poverty, they bring their religious perspective to the design of their program. As a result, poverty alleviation typically involves an encounter between Western Naturalism or Evangelical Gnosticism and the religious perspective of the materially poor people.

Sadly, it has become increasingly clear that there is something terribly wrong with the stories of change of Western civilization and the Western church, for despite our unprecedented wealth—perhaps even because of it—we are not flourishing. Disillusionment and cynicism are rampant, families and communities are breaking apart, measures of overall happiness are declining, and mental illness is skyrocketing. Many of us have reached the goal—we've achieved the American Dream in this life—but somehow this dream is far less satisfying than we thought it would be.

The tragic irony is that the implicit assumption in most of our poverty alleviation efforts is that the goal is to make poor people just like us. We try to turn Uganda into the United States and America's impoverished inner cities into its affluent suburbs. Though we are increasingly dissatisfied with our own lives, our message to poor people is "come join us!"

We need a different story of change from Western Naturalism or Evangelical Gnosticism because they aren't working. Unfortunately, most of us have been trying to live for so long in a world in which the spiritual dimension is irrelevant to our daily lives that the real world—the world of Christ's kingdom—seems quite unbelievable to us. In *Becoming Whole* chapter 5, we refer to this as Flatland—an imaginary country in which the residents' perspective is so limited to two dimensions that they can't even believe the real world has three dimensions.[6] What is a fairy tale seems real, and what is real seems like a fairy tale. As a result, we have a hard time embracing biblical principles of human flourishing and of how to achieve such flourishing. We need the Holy Spirit to open the eyes of our hearts and to infuse us with His power so that we can live into the biblical story of change, for it is the only story that really works, because it is the only story that is actually true (see Eph. 1:18–19).

Table 1.2 summarizes the different religious perspectives and stories of change of the three foundational perspectives and of Evangelical Gnosticism.

GOD'S STORY IS ALREADY COMING TRUE

Absco's diagnosis leaves him dazed and hopeless. He stops looking for work and relies on petty theft to support his growing dependence on alcohol. His story of change isn't working, but he knows of no alternative.

One day, a fellow slum dweller named Moses invites Absco to a meeting at Crossroads Church, located right in the heart of the slum. Moses explains that Crossroads has a health ministry to assist people with HIV/AIDS and a microfinance program that enables people to save and borrow money. Absco is skeptical, but he figures he has nothing to lose. So he agrees to attend the meeting at Crossroads.

When Absco and Moses enter the church, they are warmly welcomed by a group of about fifty people and offered a place to sit. Absco can tell from their accents and clothing that these people are from different tribes—tribes which don't get along with each other. Moses whispers to Absco, "This is Crossroads' savings and

TABLE 1.2

Summary of Stories of Change

		TRADITIONAL RELIGION	WESTERN NATURALISM	EVANGELICAL GNOSTICISM	HISTORIC CHRISTIANITY
THE NATURE OF:	**God**	Good and evil personal spiritual beings and impersonal spiritual forces control the physical world	Does not exist	Distant and largely disconnected from affairs of this world	Sovereign, loving, personal, and relational Being who is the Creator, Sustainer, and Reconciler of all things
	Human Beings	Similar to rest of natural world; deep spiritual connection to family, tribe, and nature	Autonomous, purely material, highly intelligent animal	Autonomous individual with separable body and soul	Highly integrated mind-affections-will-body-relational being
STORY OF CHANGE:	**What is the Goal?**	Harmony and prosperity for one's family or tribe	Material consumption	Get the soul to heaven for eternity and enjoy material consumption in this life	Serve as priest-kings whose entire being lives in right relationship with God, self, others, and rest of creation
	How is the Goal Achieved?	Manipulate the spirits to gain power	Handouts or economic growth	Evangelism to save the soul plus handouts or economic growth for the body	Through the gift of the Son and Spirit, the triune God accomplishes our reconciliation to God, self, others, and the rest of creation
THE INDIVIDUAL'S RELATIONSHIP TO:	**God**	Spirits are to be feared, appeased, and manipulated	God does not exist	Primarily legal	Intimate, loving community and worship
	Self	At the mercy of spiritual beings and forces, so has little power to affect change in world; no different from trees or animals	Center of the universe with the capacity to control the world to increase one's consumption	Soul is so valuable that Christ was willing to die to save it from eternal punishment	A priest-king uniquely created to extend the reign and worship of God
	Others	A potential threat to the harmony and prosperity of one's family or tribe	Competitors for control of material world	Other individuals who are loved at arms-length	Intimate, loving community that is served sacrificially
	Rest of Creation	Live in harmony with it rather than try to develop it	Closed machine that can be used to increase personal consumption	Closed machine that can be used to increase personal consumption	Open to actions of both humans and spiritual beings; humans should protect and develop it for God's glory

credit association. These people are just like you and me: they have migrated from different parts of the country seeking work, but now they all have HIV/AIDS." Far away from their homes, some of the group members had given in to temptations, just like Absco; others were victims of unsanitary health practices in the local clinics. Regardless, each of these people now had HIV/AIDS. As such, they are believed to be cursed by the gods, so they are treated as social outcasts.

After a time of joyful singing, the group members share their experiences.

One lady stands and says, "Hello, my name is Eunice. Jesus is my Savior. When I get my loan, I buy beads and make jewelry. I use the profits to feed my five children and to pay my rent." She sits down and then another lady speaks . . .

"Hello, my name is Margaret. I use my loan money to crochet purses out of plastic bags." Margaret then cuts several plastic grocery bags into narrow strips and crochets the strips like yarn, slowly transforming them into attractive souvenirs for tourists.

Next a tall, gaunt man stands and speaks. "When I got my loan, it was 140 Kenyan Shillings (about $2). I am an artist, and I use the fibers of the banana trees to make art. With my loan, I bought glue and I made pictures, which I sold for 3,000 Kenyan Shillings (about $43). I have two children, but my wife passed away. My profits help me to pay for my children's school expenses. I believe we should encourage one another in this program to share our talents so that our talents don't die with us."[7]

Absco stares in disbelief. Yes, in many ways these people are just like him, but in other ways they are not like him at all (see 2 Cor. 5:17):

- even though they have HIV/AIDS, they seem much healthier than others who have this deadly virus (see Luke 7:18–23)

- rather than sitting around in shame and despair, they are full of dignity and joy (see Isa. 61:3)

- instead of drowning themselves in alcohol, they have a sense of responsibility and purpose (see 1 Peter 2:9; Rev. 5:10)

- while they are from different tribes, they are putting aside their differences to form a new kind of family (see Rev. 7:9)

But to Absco, the strangest thing of all is these people's relationship with their God. Back in Absco's village, worship rituals were always a fearful attempt to appease a host of petty, self-absorbed spirits. Conversely, the people at Crossroads seem to actually enjoy being with their God, and it sounds like He wants to be with them. They praise their God for His loving care and even pray to become more like Him. *Who is this God?* Absco wonders.

The whole scene seems almost otherworldly to Absco, and indeed it is. For unbeknownst to him, he stands on holy ground. Crossroads Church is the breaking forth of the kingdom of God inside this Kenyan slum. It is the New Jerusalem of Revelation 21, the place where God Almighty dwells with His people, transported back from the future into the present. Absco has literally stumbled into the new creation, which is pushing its way up through the slum's filth and squalor, just as it did in a smelly manger two thousand years earlier. Partially, yet really, the story is already coming true.

As depicted in Figure 1.3, Crossroads embodies an alternative to the cultures of this world by creating a community whose story of change, formative practices, systems, and members reflect the kingdom of God. In the process, this community is necessarily engaged in poverty alleviation, for it is applying the power of Christ's death and resurrection to address the five causes of material poverty summarized in chapter 10 of *Becoming Whole*:

FIGURE 1.3

A Community that Embodies God's Kingdom

GOD
Demons
Story of Change
Systems
Individual Personhoods
Formative Practices
LOCAL CULTURE
MACRO CULTURE (GLOBALIZATION)

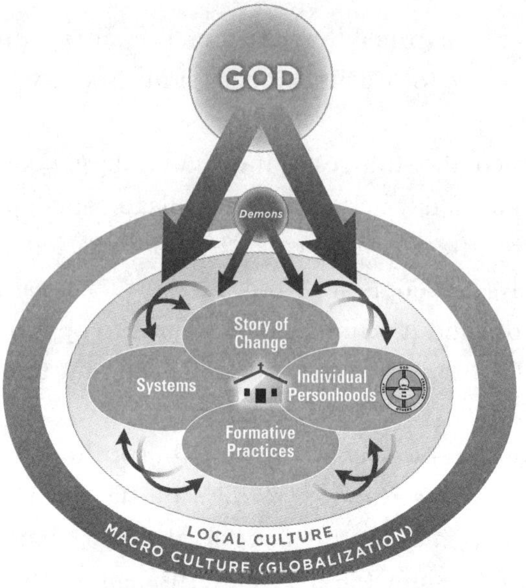

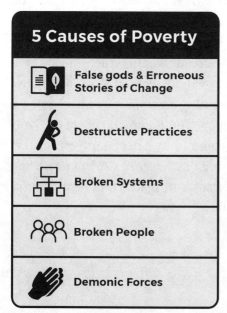

Adapted from Brian Fikkert and Michael Rhodes, "*Homo Economicus* Versus *Homo Imago Dei*," *Journal of Markets and Morality* 20, no.1 (Spring 2017): 106

5 Causes of Poverty
False gods & Erroneous Stories of Change
Destructive Practices
Broken Systems
Broken People
Demonic Forces

FIGURE 1.4

Stop and look at the list in Figure 1.4 for a moment. Is this how you think of poverty alleviation? Many of us think that poverty alleviation is about wealthy Westerners digging wells, ladling soup, or distributing backpacks. To be sure, there are circumstances in which those activities can be helpful. But the provision of these material resources usually has a lasting impact only if done in the context of the far less tangible activities in items 1 through 5 in the above list.

Crossroads' approach is working. The fact that these HIV/AIDS sufferers are operating businesses and are so full of joy is amazing to behold. But their productivity does not stop there, as each of them reports having started one to two additional savings and credit associations on their own, thereby spreading life-saving financial services, biblical teaching, fellowship, songs of praise, and prayer to roughly a thousand other people![8]

Did you catch that? These fifty modern-day "lepers" are ministering holistically to approximately a thousand other people. And God is using these restored "lepers" to declare and demonstrate His kingdom to Absco as well. The recipients of the ministry have become the advancers of the ministry.

Most of us wouldn't design a ministry this way. We wouldn't expect the beneficiaries of the ministry to actually become the ministry! Because our story of change is rooted in human power and wealth, most of us look for staff who are well-educated or have access to financial resources. Such people certainly have a role, and Crossroads uses them wisely. But in God's story of change, He uses "the foolish things," "the despised things—and the things that are not—to nullify the things that are" (1 Cor. 1:26–29). The kingdom of God is upside down, so at the very bottom—which is mysteriously at the very top—are lepers restored as priest-kings, new creatures in Christ who are spreading the reign and worship of God in the most unlikely places.[9]

WHAT'S THE SECRET FORMULA?

The remainder of the book articulates the underlying principles that the Chalmers Center uses to design ministries like the one we helped Crossroads Church start. The hope is that these Ministry Design Principles can provide at least some help to pastors, elders, deacons, boards, ministry leaders, staff, volunteers, and donors to promote more effective poverty alleviation ministries at home or abroad across a wide spectrum: health care, education, human trafficking, clean water, homelessness, jobs preparedness, and so on.

It is with much trepidation that we put forth these Ministry Design Principles. Neither we authors nor the Chalmers Center as a whole have this all figured out. Poverty alleviation is extremely complex, and there is considerable mystery to how God's world works. Many times, we are just completely wrong. Moreover, even when we do have the right ideas, a gap always exists between the theory of what we are doing and the actual practice on the ground. Like all organizations, the Chalmers Center and its ministry partners are full of broken and finite people.

Even when we do get it right, we don't claim that these principles are unique to us. We stand on the shoulders of many others who have influenced us through their research, experience, writing, speaking, mentoring, and partnership. Hence, what follows should *not* be considered as "the Chalmers Center's answers." Rather, they should be treated as a diary of our imperfect gleanings from the wisdom of many others who have helped us along the way, gleanings that we hope will be helpful to others.

While these principles reflect the insights of many wise people, they are not a magic formula. *There simply is no one-size-fits-all recipe that is guaranteed to move people out of poverty.* Readers will need to pray for godly wisdom to know how to apply these principles in their particular contexts.

It is extremely likely that the ministries with which you are involved already incorporate some of the Ministry Design Principles in this *Field Guide,* but it is also quite possible that some of the concepts presented here will be very new to you. In fact, some of the principles may sound downright strange to you, so strange that you may wonder whether they actually work. The good news is that these principles have been used by ministries to improve the lives of millions of poor people just like Absco, and scientific evidence supports many of them. But ultimately neither practical experience nor scientific research is the ultimate standard. Rather, we believe the Bible tells us much about human flourishing and how God is working to achieve such flourishing. While we can observe some of this process, most of the biblical story is spiritual, unmeasurable, and incomprehensible. So, ultimately, we must accept this story by faith—faith that God is real, that His Word is trustworthy, and that He always keeps His promises, including His promises to use His means to make His people whole.

It is important to emphasize that the Chalmers Center did *not* make the HIV/AIDS ministry work. Far more credit goes to Crossroads Church, which is the primary manifestation of God's kingdom in the Kenyan slum. It is this church that provided the vision, resources, and wisdom needed to launch this ministry; and it is this church's faithful sacrifices that keep it going.

And ultimately, all glory goes to God. Poverty alleviation is not fundamentally about correctly applying principles, techniques, and methods, as important as those are. Rather, successful poverty alleviation depends on God to supernaturally intervene in His world, and He is not subject to human manipulation. God is the central actor in His own story of change.

Our dependence on God does not imply that we do nothing, passively waiting for God to act. Rather, because we have been restored as the royal priesthood and the holy nation, we are called to faithfully live into God's story of change, dynamically working with Him to advance His kingdom. And because God hasn't given us a detailed script, we need to improvise our roles in His unfolding drama.

Our hope is that this *Field Guide* will serve as a prompt for this improvisation, providing some direction for all of us as we experiment with the best way to apply God's story in our various contexts. Although we should take care not to hurt others, the reality is that we will make all kinds of mistakes along the way. This reality should not paralyze us. Rather, we should move forward in both humility and joy, knowing that—despite our failures—the triune God will make His story break forth into this world, both for materially poor people and for ourselves.

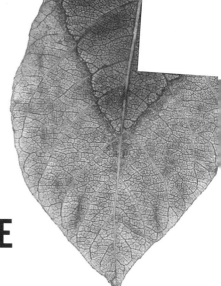

CHAPTER TWO

FORMING THE COMMUNITY OF THE KINGDOM OF GOD

The Church on earth . . . is not merely a promise or pledge of the heavenly Church, but is an anticipation of it. The Holy Spirit, the eschatological gift, has already been poured forth on the Christian community.[1]

—AVERY DULLES, THEOLOGIAN, 2002

This is the sense in which we practice resurrection—we engage in a life that is permeated by the presence and companionship of the resurrected Jesus in the company of friends.[2]

—EUGENE PETERSON, THEOLOGIAN, 2006

A s the royal priesthood and holy nation, God's people are called to form a community that applies the power of Christ's death and resurrection to live into the new creation. Although in some ways this community is distinct from the surrounding culture, it should not look inward, cloistering itself off from the world. On the contrary, because Christ is King of the entire cosmos, this community should seek to extend the knowledge of His presence and reign across every square inch of His domain (2 Cor. 5:16–21; 1 Peter 2:9). As shown in Figure 2.1, Christians do this in three arenas, as we discussed in *Becoming Whole* chapter 10:

First, there are some things the Bible indicates that the church should do *directly*: preach the Word, administer the sacraments, exercise discipline, engage in fellowship, and care for the poor, especially poor believers (Gal. 2:10).[3] When the church engages in these activities, it *directly* ministers holistically to the people in its midst.

Second, some believers are called to be involved in parachurch ministries, which explicitly seek to help the church fulfill its mission by undertaking tasks that are beyond the capacity of the local church. Many poverty alleviation ministries fall into this category. Some parachurch ministries may be national or even international in scope (some Christian relief and development agencies, for example) while others will be much more local.

Third, some believers are called to serve as priest-kings in institutions that are not parachurch ministries in that they are not engaged in explicitly Christian ministry (such as government, business, the arts, and civic organizations). While these institutions are not rooted in the local church, Christ is the Creator, Sustainer, and Reconciler of all things, including these institutions, so Christians must work in them as well, faithfully seeking to use words and deeds that bear witness to the present and future reign of Christ as much as possible (Matt. 5:16; Col. 1:15–20).

FIGURE 2.1

The Church, Parachurch, and Larger Society

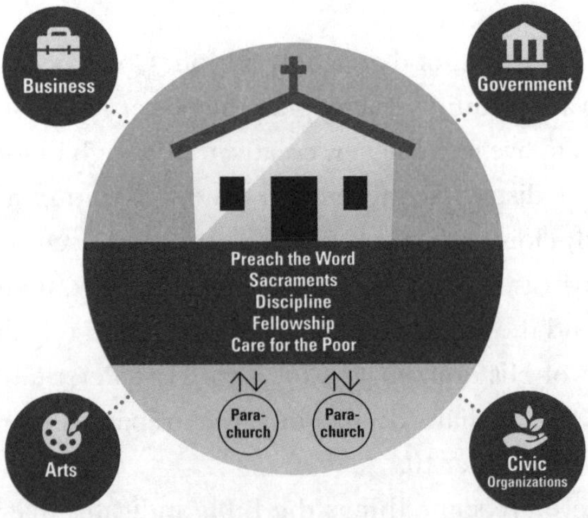

Adapted from Fig. 6.5 in Bryant L. Myers, *Walking with the Poor: Principles and Practices of Transformational Development*, rev. ed. (Maryknoll, NY: Orbis, 2011), 199.

Throughout His earthly ministry, Jesus displayed a special concern for the materially poor, wanting them to enjoy the benefits of His kingdom (Luke 4:18–21; 7:18–23). So while the kingdom community should seek the flourishing of the entire creation, it ought to have a particular concern for those who are materially poor. Toward that end, the remainder of this *Field Guide* articulates Ministry Design Principles that can foster a community that applies the power of Christ's death and resurrection to address the five causes of poverty, as depicted in Figure 2.2.[4]

Although Christians should be active in all three of the arenas mentioned earlier, in keeping with the focus of this book, the discussion will focus on the first two arenas: the church and parachurch ministries.

While the focus of the discussion will be on helping materially poor people, these principles apply to all of us because we all are in the process of becoming whole. We need to remove the mindset that says, "We are okay, but materially poor people are not okay, so we are designing a ministry to help them become just like us." Rather, we should say, "We are all broken, and this brokenness bubbles up

FIGURE 2.2

in different ways in our lives. This means that we need to find ways to apply God's story of change in our own lives even as we help materially poor people to apply it in theirs." In this light, try to think about the implications of the Ministry Design Principles, not just for poverty alleviation ministries, but for your own process of becoming whole.

THE KINGDOM COMMUNITY: FORMING THE COMMUNITY

Kingdom Community

Ministry Design Principle 1: Christian poverty alleviation ministries must be "rooted in and lead back to" the local church.

Human beings are created to live in God's presence, so at the center of the kingdom community is the palace of the King, the place where He dwells and from which He rules in the here and now: the local church. In this light, arguably one of the primary metrics for determining the success of any poverty alleviation ministry is this: *Are the church and ministry functioning in such a way that materially poor people long to be present with God's people for corporate worship on Sunday morning?* And a corollary metric is this: *Are our churches welcoming and culturally accessible to poor people?*

Worship and Poverty Alleviation

Human beings are transformed into the image of whatever god they worship, so at the core of poverty alleviation is worship of the one true God.

These metrics present quite a challenge for most of our ministries. Many of our churches don't even know any poor people, and the culture of our congregations and our corporate worship create tremendous barriers for them. Moreover, while parachurch ministries definitely have a role to play in poverty alleviation, they often are not connected to the local church. Bryant Myers captures the frustrations that many parachurch staff have with local churches, a frustration that he laments:

> Too often Christian development professionals see
> the church as a distraction, or worse, an impediment
> to transformation. "The church has separated itself
> from the rest of the community." "Churches don't
> believe development is something they should be
> doing." "The church is not professional enough;

it doesn't know what it is doing." "Churches have
been validating the current economic and political
system; they are part of the problem." We know the
litany well.[5]

To be sure, there is truth in each of the frustrations expressed in
this quote. Churches often lack a kingdom vision that includes ministering to low-income individuals and communities, and even when
they capture such a vision, their approaches often do more harm
than good. The church needs to deeply understand and consistently
live out the biblical story of change, not the story of Evangelical
Gnosticism.

That having been said, the parachurch has its own problems.
Indeed, perhaps the lack of connection between the church and the
parachurch is at least partly due to parachurches having erroneous
views of the nature of human beings and of how God is working in the
world, making them undervalue what the local church brings to the
table in poverty alleviation. In other words, perhaps parachurches do
not really understand the biblical story of change either; perhaps they
too fail to understand the process of becoming whole.

Ask any staff worker in a parachurch ministry the following question: *What does the Lord's Supper have to do with poverty alleviation?* You
are likely to get bewildered stares. Indeed, you might find this question to be a bit strange yourself!

That this question sounds so strange to our ears is just one manifestation of the many ways Evangelical Gnosticism has so deeply
impacted us. Remember, Evangelical Gnosticism views human beings
as "brains on sticks": the body and the soul are seen as separable,
and the soul is often treated as nothing more than the mind. Similarly, Evangelical Gnosticism often reduces the Lord's Supper to a
purely cognitive experience in which we try to get our brains to stop
daydreaming in order to remember Christ's death. As a result, when
many evangelicals receive the Lord's Supper, they believe that—at
most—their brains are being impacted. But God is doing more than
merely offering a history lesson in this sacrament. He actually feeds

and nourishes His people in their whole being, offering Himself to them in a particular way that comes only through this church-based sacrament.[6] More is happening in the Lord's Supper than what one receives from reading a book.

A biblical anthropology sees human beings as integrated mind-affections-will-body-relational creatures. So, for example, what happens to us spiritually and relationally impacts us physically, and vice versa. There seems to be a reason the sacraments instituted by Christ have a physical reality to them (bread, wine, water). Admitting this doesn't have to mean we imagine the physical elements of the bread and wine actually change or turn into something besides bread and wine (though some traditions do believe that). But it does mean we should be cautious about failing to imagine *something* is happening in this special event that is celebrated by God's people.

Historical Christianity, in its various expressions, teaches that Christ is mysteriously but really present *in* the "ordinary means of grace"—the preaching of the Word, the administration of the sacraments, and prayer. When the Word is preached and the bread and the wine are administered, the risen Christ Himself is present and is being offered to us so that our entire being is being nurtured in our union with Him. As John Calvin imagined it, for example, by faith believers are elevated into the heavens as they partake of the Lord's Supper, giving them a taste of being with Christ who Himself says, through the minister, "This is my body given for you" (Luke 22:19). It is actually *Christ* speaking to us through the minister. By *faith, Christ* is present, or, we are present *with Christ*: in this Supper, believers genuinely receive from God needed grace, comfort, and strength. The Supper is a distinctive means of grace and not merely a help for our struggling minds.[7]

Certainly, this is a cognitive experience, but it is so much more than that! The woman who had been bleeding for twelve years knew who Jesus was, but she needed more than just abstract knowledge: she needed healing, and she needed the Healer—not just the idea of Him, but *Him* (Luke 8:43–48). So she pushed her way through the crowd to touch Jesus, the King whose flesh—yes, even whose cloak—carries in it the power to overturn all of the effects of the Fall, bringing healing to our minds, affections, wills, bodies, and relationships. Our entire beings—indeed, all of creation—long to touch the Healer. And in the ordinary means of grace, He mysteriously reaches out and draws us to Himself; here He touches us, every dimension of who we are, penetrating even to our deepest needs. In this experience of communion, we are returned to the dwelling place of God.

Jesus Himself *is* the temple, so as we take Him in through hearing the Word and eating the bread and the wine, we experience being in the temple and the temple being in us, not just in our brains but in our entire mind-affections-will-body-relational personhoods. And in communion with God we are also pointed back toward restored communion with our neighbors. Brought back into God's presence, the top spoke in the wheel is restored, and we experience something more of what it means to be whole. *This is poverty alleviation!*

FIGURE 2.3

The Restoration of the Human Being

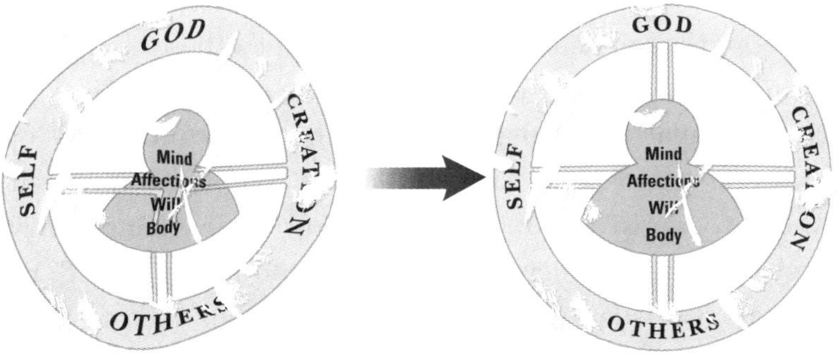

Adapted from Brian Fikkert and Russell Mask, *From Dependence to Dignity: How to Alleviate Poverty through Church-Centered Microfinance* (Grand Rapids: Zondervan, 2015), 91.

So what does the Lord's Supper have to do with poverty alleviation? Everything! There is simply no substitute. It is for this reason that theologian Leslie Newbigin states: parachurch ministries "have power to accomplish their purpose only as they are rooted in and lead back to a believing community," the community of the local church.[8]

Does this all seem mysterious? It is. But that doesn't make it any less true.

Does it sound impossible for the parachurch to be "rooted in and lead back to" the local church? It isn't, as evidenced by the microfinance ministry of Crossroads Church described in chapter 1. The savings and credit association is actually owned and operated by the fifty HIV/AIDS sufferers. They set the rules for the group, they select their own officers, they run the meetings, and they save and lend their own money to one another. It's a parachurch ministry led by materially poor people who are members of Crossroads Church and who see this ministry as "rooted in and lead back to" it.

The key to making this possible is the question we asked when the Chalmers Center first began designing microfinance ministries two decades ago: *How can we help Majority World churches declare and demonstrate the good news of God's kingdom by helping poor people glorify God through sustaining work?* Framing the question this way set important boundaries on the types of ministries that could be designed.

First, there were an insufficient number of jobs in these settings, so we turned to microfinance and microenterprise development to help people be self-employed. Second, we knew these churches and their members were very poor and had little education. They didn't have the capacity—managerial, human, or financial—to operate large programs, especially not ones as complex as most microfinance programs. Third, there are a host of problems in having churches manage money such as savings and loans. Indeed, many large-scale, Christian microfinance organizations tried to discourage us, telling us that their worst clients were churches, whose pastors and members seemed to believe that "grace" meant loans didn't need to be repaid.

What to do? God led one of the founding members of the Chalmers Center, Dr. Russell Mask, to a solution. For a variety of technical reasons, savings and credit associations are much simpler to operate than the huge programs that most NGOs were running, programs whose methodology required educated leadership staff, lots of outside capital, highly sophisticated systems, and thousands of clients. In contrast, with only a little training, even very poor people can own and operate savings and credit associations using their own managerial, human, financial, social, and spiritual resources. So, the Chalmers Center developed training and curriculum that Majority World churches could use to foster savings and credit associations, teaching the churches to set these up as parachurch ministries to avoid the problems of mixing microfinance with the local church. But unlike many parachurch ministries, these are so closely connected to the church that the pastors, church members, volunteers, group members, and surrounding culture see them as a ministry of the church that fostered them and that continues to nurture them.

By God's grace and the outstanding work of partners such as Compassion International, Five Talents, HOPE International, Saddleback Church, and Tearfund, some of the poorest churches in the world have been equipped to reach hundreds of thousands of people through church-centered savings and credit associations over the past twenty years. One thing that excites us most is that—in contrast to many poverty alleviation efforts—the local churches with which we and our partners work have a strong sense of "ownership" of these ministries, even though they don't actually own them in a legal sense. These are *their ministries,* not the ministries of the outside organizations. It really is possible to create parachurch ministries that are "rooted in and lead back to" the local church, even when the churches are extremely poor.

Again, the key to all this was the question we asked up front: *How can we help Majority World churches declare and demonstrate the good news of God's kingdom by helping poor people glorify God through sustaining work?* This question framed everything:

- The focus on *Majority World churches* required us to grapple theologically with what the Bible teaches about the mission of the local church and to design an intervention that was within the capacity of these churches to implement.

- The *declaring and demonstrating* phrase required an approach that kept the words and deeds of the gospel in balance and highly integrated with one another. This had huge implications for the design of our training and curriculum, for the nature of our distributors, and for the types of funding sources that we could use.

- The message of *God's kingdom* required training and curriculum that communicate how Christ's lordship governs every aspect of people's lives, not simply how they can get their souls saved.

- The emphasis on helping *poor people* directed virtually every feature of program design: choice of intervention, training, curricula, type of churches, and so on.

- The focus on *work* ruled out a host of other interventions that are more popular and much easier to implement—such as feeding programs or short-term trips.

- The goal of *glorifying God* meant that the training and curriculum needed to include more than technical information. It also needed to narrate the purpose of work and its connection to glorifying God, and it emphasized the need to ask God to help us achieve these purposes.

If we had started with a different question—like, *How can we quickly provide financial services to as many poor people as possible?*—we would have designed a completely different program. It would have been much more sophisticated and would have reached far more people. And it also would have been much more dependent on outside managerial, human, and financial resources, and far less holistic and completely disconnected from the local church.

The point we are trying to make is *not* that there is no role for such large-scale programs. Indeed, they have the potential to do a lot of good. Rather, the point here is that how one designs a program—and the types of impact that the program has—flows out of one's explicit or implicit story of change. Because we believe that the local church is central to God's story of change—both in terms of His goals and His way of achieving those goals—it took us down a different path and gave us very different outcomes from those we would have had otherwise. And by God's grace alone, the result is that a small church is better equipped to be the infusion of the kingdom of God in a Kenyan slum, and fifty modern-day lepers are restored priest-kings who are serving a thousand other people.

Questions for Reflection:
1. What is your own degree of commitment to the local church?

_____

_____

_____

_____

2. What can your poverty alleviation ministry do to increase the desire of materially poor people to become full participants in a local church?

_____

_____

_____

_____

3. What adjustments might need to be made to your church's culture—attitudes, décor, dress, worship, preaching, teaching, demographics, or even location—in order for materially poor people to be welcomed as full participants into the life of the church?

_____

_____

_____

_____

Kingdom Community

Ministry Design Principle 2: Use supportive, gospel-centered groups as much as possible.

Human beings are deeply wired for community—the "relationship with others" spoke in the wheel. In fact, community precedes work: God existed in community before He acted in creating the world, and He has wired human beings in the same way.[9] But note also that work is to be done in community. "The LORD God said, 'It is not good for the man to be alone. I will make a helper suitable for him'" (Gen. 2:18). Note in this verse that community is not just for the weekend. Adam and Eve were co-laborers. The two of them worked, in community, to fulfill their calling as priest-kings. Hence, we need community not just on Sunday, but Monday through Saturday as well.

Although this is true for all people, it is particularly true for materially poor people, who often experience the following:

- Geographic, social, and economic isolation

- Lack of support and encouragement

- Feelings of shame and loneliness

- Messages that they are inferior and worthless

In this light, try to use supportive and encouraging groups as much as possible in the design of your ministry. For example, in the interests of efficiency, many microfinance programs are moving away from methodologies that require groups of poor people to meet, sometimes even collecting savings and administering loans to individuals via cell phones, thereby removing the need for any human interaction. While this approach cuts down on time and costs, it also loses the tremendous power of the group, so the Chalmers Center continues to use the group-based approach in its microfinance ministries. Yes, cell phones would be more efficient—and there is sometimes a role for them—but "God sets the lonely in families" (Ps. 68:6). Indeed, commenting on the microfinance ministry of Crossroads

Church, a community health worker remarks, "Most of these people have been ostracized by their families and have come from all over the country to this slum. The fact that people from different tribes have come together and formed a new 'family' is an amazing thing."[10]

Similarly, Saddleback Church uses group-based approaches in its microfinance ministry in Rwanda. A leader at Saddleback asked the savings and credit association members about the impact on their lives:[11]

> After the genocide I was a lonely person. I belonged nowhere. I started going to church and heard about the savings groups. The group helped me to build my farm from a small plot into a bigger farm and profitable business. I can now buy health insurance for my family. This group has become my family and has resurrected me.
>
> —*Beatrice, a genocide survivor*

> My life has been transformed. I used to be poor and was ashamed to go out in public. But now, through my church and my savings group, God has blessed my family. I have gone from subsistence farming to owning a restaurant. We have food, school fees, and health insurance. We have enough to give offerings to the church. The church is our second family. I am no longer ashamed to go out.
>
> —*Clementine, a wife and mother of seven*

Notice in these testimonies the power of the group in removing loneliness and isolation, in overcoming shame, and in providing the foundation that launches people into sustaining work.

Groups that are supportive and encouraging act like a greenhouse, a habitat that shields people from the harsh external environment and provides them with a context in which they can heal and flourish. Recall that as malleable mind-affections-will-body-relational creatures, human beings can be damaged by external forces, just as wheels can be damaged by potholes. As we discovered in *Becoming Whole* chapter 7, oppressive systems and harmful narratives can do lasting damage to every aspect of the mind-affections-will-body-relational creature. For many poor people, the explicit or implicit messages of the culture communicate: "You'll never amount to anything;" "People from your race are good-for-nothings;" or "Women aren't as good as men. " In such cases, there is tremendous healing power in being part of a group that is singing a different tune, the tune of the gospel of the kingdom: "God loves you, and so do we; you are of infinite value and have something to contribute; you are part of our family, so welcome home!"

In addition, groups can provide the loving accountability that we all need. Ongoing change is central to becoming whole, and change is always hard. We all need people who can speak into our lives, lovingly correcting us when we are wrong and spurring us on to love and good deeds (Heb. 10:24; James 5:20).

Finally, if any members of the group are *not* materially poor, they can often make the systems work better for those who are. Materially poor people typically lack access to valuable social networks that we take for granted, so we can help by connecting them to our friends: business owners, landlords, and bankers who can assist with jobs, housing, and loans. Moreover, as we walk with materially poor people over time, we will discover systems that are broken or unjust, creating opportunities for us to use our influence to advocate for much-needed systemic change. And in the process, we will start to see how life looks through their eyes, making us more empathetic people—making us more whole.

In fact, supportive groups can be so powerful that—in addition to being a component of a ministry—they can actually be *the ministry*. Such is the case with the circles of support model in which a team of two to five allies, who are typically not materially poor, come alongside the circle leader, a materially poor individual. The circle leader articulates their group's goals and what they will do to achieve those goals, and then the allies offer encouragement, support, accountability, and help with accessing social networks and navigating systems. Joy Barnhill shares the impact of this model in her own life:

> It wasn't until I was an adult that I realized I grew up poor. Poverty was all I knew. As a kid, a special treat for me would have been a little box of grape juice.
>
> I have a learning disability, so I was bounced around several schools. I wanted to learn, but it was always hard. I didn't know why I couldn't learn as well as all the other kids. Today I read at a fifth grade level. My teachers told me I wouldn't amount to much. Imagine how that affects your self-esteem as a child. It destroys your confidence, your ambition, your hope.
>
> People aren't always poor because they are lazy. A lot of times they are just a product of their environment. Self-confidence? A good work ethic? Saving money? Those things have to be taught. If no one teaches those things to you as a child, you already have two strikes against you as an adult. And that was pretty much how my life went until I was 31, a cycle of just getting by.

Then a friend encouraged Joy to join the circles of support ministry that is part of the ACTS initiative of Fairhaven Church and Think Tank of Dayton, Ohio.[12] Joy continues,

> For the first time, I met people who believed in me. Instead of hearing, "You'll never amount to anything," I started hearing, "You can do this" and "Things can be different." I was partnered with several mentors (allies) who became my good friends. They taught me things I had never learned. Things as simple as how to dress for a job interview, make eye contact in an interview, and how to budget money.

Over the course of 18 months they helped me set goals and walked beside me to help me achieve them. But they also loved me for who I was. During this time, one of the pastors led me to Christ.

This movement is not about giving poor people a handout. It's about giving them a hand up, teaching them how to climb out of poverty and cheering them on as they go. I'm so thankful for all these people. Without their friendship and their commitment to helping me succeed, I wouldn't be where I am today.

It hasn't been easy, and I've still got a long way to go. But I'm on my way. I know how to get to my next goal, and I have people encouraging me to get there. That makes such a difference. Those people don't look at me and just see a poor person or someone with no future. They see me as Jesus sees me: some-one worth dying for. . . . My name is Joy Barnhill, and I am the proud owner of Joy-Full Cleaning.[13]

Questions for Reflection:
1. How do you feel when you are lacking a supportive community?

_____
_____
_____
_____

2. What could you do to make greater use of supportive and encouraging groups in your poverty alleviation ministry?

_____
_____
_____
_____

3. Are there any ways that you could foster healthy groups that include both materially poor and materially non-poor people? For example, consider the circles of support model in this chapter or the *Faith & Finances* communities described in the next chapter.

_____

_____

_____

_____

CHAPTER THREE

CONQUERING FALSE GODS AND ERRONEOUS STORIES OF CHANGE

> [Worship of money] causes men to be more concerned about making a living than making a life. This is the danger forever threatening our capitalistic economy which places so much emphasis on the profit motive. . . . There is the danger in such a system that men will become so involved in the money getting process that they will unconsciously forget to pursue those great eternal values which make life worth living.[1]
>
> —MARTIN LUTHER KING JR., PASTOR AND CIVIL RIGHTS LEADER, 1953

> When I have money, I get rid of it quickly, lest it find a way into my heart.[2]
>
> —JOHN WESLEY, FOUNDER OF METHODISM, 18TH CENTURY

I was doing five years' prison time out in Phoenix, Arizona. When I came out, I went through a year's discipleship program. . . . I came home [to Atlanta], and I was homeless. I found a shelter and stayed there. I wasn't using [drugs] anymore, and I knew I needed a spiritual house, I needed a church. So my first week there, I walked up to the corner, and that's how I found North Avenue [Presbyterian Church]. I walked in, and I told the Lord, 'I'm going to go back out. Lead me where I need to be.' That's where He told me to 'sit my butt down,' and that's where it's been ever since."[3]

North Avenue Presbyterian Church, right in the heart of midtown Atlanta, welcomed Maurice. But it wasn't sure how to help him and the many others in similar situations on its doorsteps. The church invited Maurice to attend its Sunday School class for people who were homeless and recovering from addictions, but what else could they be doing?

Things began to change when North Avenue hired Matt Seadore as Director of Missions and Outreach. Matt explains, "[Our church] had a lot of programs for people who are materially poor, but there wasn't a whole lot of relational connection. It was a whole lot more about doing 'for', rather than being 'with'. . . . I saw really early on that Maurice was like a person of peace, that he could be a bridge who could connect me to the materially poor community."

Matt and his family began hosting pancake suppers for some of the materially poor people who were connected to the church, including Maurice. During one of those suppers, Maurice told his whole life story—about growing up in the segregated South, having abusive parents, becoming homeless, and having three extended stays in three different state penitentiaries.

Matt recalls, "We were just amazed at hearing all that and the trust that Maurice had given to us, by sharing that with us." Prompted by his young daughter, Matt realized that he hadn't extended that same trust to Maurice. While Maurice had shared everything about himself, Matt hadn't even been open with him about the awkwardness he'd felt in opening his home and trying to get conversations started. Matt continues, "the next week . . . I pulled Maurice aside. . . . I confessed that I suffered from what I'd call ambivalent hospitality—I'll wave you in with one arm and hold you at a safe distance with the other one. In that space, repentance and forgiveness embraced, and it just changed the trajectory of our friendship. It freed something inside of me that allowed Maurice to be a deep soul friend of mine."

Maurice adds, "It just shows you how the Spirit of God works, because it's not ever about you and your uncomfortableness. It's in your uncomfortableness that you will be allowed to grow."

Matt and Maurice have been able to grow in relationship through serving together, including implementing the Chalmers Center's *Faith & Finances* ministry, which fosters relationships across socioeconomic lines while learning about biblical principles of financial stewardship. Maurice testifies, "Three years ago I had no bank account, no credit cards, no sense of security financially, even though I still had peace and I knew God was at work. From then to now I got a vehicle. I got a truck that I own. I pay the insurance. I have a maintenance fund for that truck. I have a 'blow fund'. . . . I got financial security. I've been more socially connected through personal relationships through it. . . . *Faith & Finances* has definitely made a difference in my life and my world. It gave me hope. It's a part of me being free." Matt adds, *Faith & Finances* "has created a relational glue that wasn't there in our congregation before."

But God wasn't done yet. As Matt explains, "We really started to look at, as a church, how we would grow in that idea of 'being with.' I began to challenge the church that we have things to learn from those who are materially poor, and if we value them as we say we value them, we need to give a seat at the leadership table to someone from that community. At that time, Maurice was named a deacon in our church, and he's now been asked to re-up for a second three-year term."

"Maurice doesn't let us get away with anything. What he brings to the mission leadership team is just brutal honesty. His being part of [that team] has been an important corrective to where we would naturally go . . . He brings a different perspective to the table in important conversations."

The church's neighborhood is changing rapidly due to the city's new policies toward homelessness. As North Avenue learns how to navigate the next steps, Maurice has been appointed to a church task force about how to respond to these changes, and he has been hired full-time as a counselor and advocate by an organization that is working with homeless persons.

God has chosen the lowly and the despised things to become priest-kings in His kingdom (see 1 Cor. 1:20–26), and they are being equipped and sent forth from His dwelling places, places like North Avenue Presbyterian Church in midtown Atlanta.

THE KINGDOM COMMUNITY:
CONQUERING FALSE GODS AND ERRONEOUS STORIES OF CHANGE

Living faithfully as the royal priesthood and holy nation entails calling on King Jesus to overcome all the effects of the Fall, including all five causes of poverty. The previous chapter discussed the formation of the community itself, and this chapter focuses on how the community can fight against false gods and erroneous stories of change.

As we saw in *Becoming Whole* chapter 2, human beings and societies are transformed into the image of whatever god they worship. So, it is essential that the community of the kingdom is centered on worship of King Jesus, the only God whose qualities are consistent with human flourishing, consistent with being whole.

The kingdom community inaugurates its worship each week in the local church, the place where God dwells and from which He rules. Worship then continues throughout the week as the restored priest-kings offer their entire lives as living sacrifices to their King (Rom. 12:1). As we engage in this week-long worship, we are "transformed into his image with ever-increasing glory" through His Spirit (2 Cor. 3:18). We begin to love the way that King Jesus loves in all our relationships: we start to garden the way He gardens, to build the way He builds, to hug the way He hugs, and to rest the way that He rests. And as this happens, we increasingly become who we are created to be. We become whole.

As we go forth to work in Christ's kingdom, we must recognize that because Jesus is King, His story of change, not the erroneous stories of the false gods, is the only one that actually works in His realm. In other words, King Jesus' goals and His way of achieving those goals amount to the "laws of nature," the rules by which the universe actually operates in His new creation. Hence, if we truly want to alleviate poverty, if we truly want people to become whole, our ministries must be designed in ways that are consistent with King Jesus' story of change, not with the erroneous stories of change of Western Naturalism, Evangelical Gnosticism, or traditional religion.

In *Becoming Whole*, we reinforce these ideas by repeated use of the following three boxes:

Worship and Poverty Alleviation

Human beings are transformed into the image of whatever god they worship, so at the core of poverty alleviation is worship of the one true God.

The Goal of God's Story of Change

*People experience human flourishing **when they serve as priest-kings**, using their mind, affections, will, and body to enjoy loving relationships with God, self, others, and the rest of creation.*

The Way to Achieve the Goal of God's Story of Change

Through the gift of the Son and Spirit, the triune God accomplishes our reconciliation to God, self, others, and the rest of creation.

Unfortunately, we all have been deeply influenced by false gods and their erroneous stories of change. Hence, the content of these boxes is completely foreign to the vast majority of poverty alleviation efforts and to our lives in general. Most of us have been trying to live in the imaginary world of Flatland for so long that the real world—the world of Christ's kingdom—seems quite unbelievable to us. As a result, we find it difficult to live into God's story of change.

In this light, effective poverty alleviation requires enormous faith. All the stakeholders of the ministry—*the board, leadership, staff, volunteers, financial supporters, and materially poor people*—need to trust that human flourishing consists not in ever-increasing consumption but in enjoying loving relationships with God, self, others, and the rest of the creation. And all the stakeholders need to trust that Jesus Christ is the only One who can enable such flourishing to happen, both for the materially poor and for all of us.

What does this look like in daily life? In particular, how can poverty alleviation ministries encourage all their stakeholders to worship God throughout the week and to walk in light of His story of change? There is no one-size-fits-all recipe, but there are several principles that can help us as we improvise together.

Story
Conquering false gods and erroneous stories of truth

Ministry Design Principle 3: All the ministry stakeholders should "pray without ceasing."
Worshiping God and walking with Him throughout the week includes regularly communicating with Him. The primary way that God speaks to us is through His Word, and then we respond by speaking to Him in prayer. Somehow this praying is to be "without ceasing" (1 Thess. 5:17 ESV), which can include pausing from our activities to offer up prayers as well as praying "under our breath" as we send emails, go to meetings, and sweep the floor. Unfortunately, because Evangelical Gnosticism has conditioned us to believe that God is inactive in His world, many of us struggle to see the point of such ongoing prayer, or even know how to do it.

It is also interesting to note that while many ministries have a full-time Director of Development (fundraising), very few have a full-time Director of Prayer. Such a position sounds strange, doesn't it? What would happen if we asked our donors to fund such a position? And what would happen if our ministries spent even a fraction of the time we spend on planning, marketing, and fundraising on reading the Word and prayer?

To be sure, development staff are both necessary and good. Ministries need funds to operate, and helping God's people to experience the joy of generosity is a very high calling. Indeed, the Triune

God expresses His love via lavish generosity, and as His image bearers we are called to do the same.

But perhaps our staffing, time allocation, and budgets reveal something about the story of change that actually governs our ministries. If we are living in Flatland Monday through Saturday—as both Western Naturalism and Evangelical Gnosticism believe—then our current *modus operandi* is just fine. But given that Flatland isn't real, perhaps we need to rethink the design of our organizations. And ideally, there is not just one person praying, but the development officers, teachers, custodians, and all involved are encouraged to cultivate a spirit of prayer throughout all areas of their lives and work.

New Generations, a ministry that fosters Disciple Making Movements (DMM) in some of the most difficult regions of the world, reports that since 2005 it has seen over 61,000 new churches planted comprising 1.5 million new disciples.[4] When asked what advice he would give to similar ministries, Harry Brown, the President of New Generations, responds:

> Prayer is absolutely fundamental to the DMM work.
> If you neglect this, you will never release the power
> to break the strongholds and set the captives free.
> Many organizations never get momentum in DMM
> because they don't really recognize the absolute
> necessity of abundant prayer in the beginning and
> throughout the process. We would advise our fellow
> ministries to not only make this the cornerstone of
> their strategy but to invest a significant part of their
> budget in mobilizing and training intercessors.[5]

New Generations currently spends 10 percent of its operating budget on mobilizing and equipping prayer intercessors for their work. Their five-year goal is to increase the number of such intercessors from 10,000 to 100,000.[6] Unfortunately, the approach of New Generations is all too rare. Many of our ministries fail to live out the following verses:

Some trust in chariots and some in horses,
　　but we trust in the name of the LORD our God.
They are brought to their knees and fall,
　　but we rise up and stand firm. (Ps. 20:7–8)

Can we really say we embrace the truths in these verses when so much of our work relies on our own strength?

Similarly, do our ministries communicate to materially poor people that the key to their advancement ultimately rests on their ability to become more disciplined, to pull themselves up by their own bootstraps, to get more education, and to work harder? Yes, materially poor people need to take actions to improve their situations. But as we walk with them through this process, we must constantly communicate that poverty alleviation is ultimately an act of King Jesus, urging them to cry out to Him and His Spirit for help in overcoming all the obstacles—both internal and external—that they face every day, even as we learn to do the same.

Questions for Reflection:

1. What role does prayer play in your personal life?

_____

_____

_____

_____

2. Think about where resources are allocated in your ministry. What does this imply about your organization's story of change?

_____

_____

_____

_____

3. What specific actions could you take to increase the role of prayer in your ministry?

_____

_____

_____

_____

Story

Conquering false gods and erroneous stories of truth

Ministry Design Principle 4: Narrate God's story of change throughout life.

God has wired human beings in such a way that we need to be exposed to a constant narration of God's story of change, lest we adopt the story of change of the surrounding culture.[7] We need to be discipled how to enjoy loving relationships with God, self, others, and the rest of creation throughout our daily lives, and we need to learn to call on King Jesus and the power of His indwelling Spirit for help in doing so. Remember, the stories of change of the world have encultured us to *automatically* and often *unconsciously* live in ways that are inconsistent with Christ's kingdom. Hence, we need to be immersed in a new song and to dance a new dance, reorienting our minds, affections, wills, and bodies as we work, play, eat, and sleep.

The narration of God's story needs to begin each week with the formal gathering of the church for its weekly worship in the restored temple. The prayers, songs, preaching, and sacraments need to tell the story of the gospel of the kingdom of God, not the false gospel of Evangelical Gnosticism. People need to understand that death has no more power over King Jesus or us, that we share in His resurrection life *right now*, and that He is restoring the entire creation to all that it was created to be. In addition to taking care of the Law's accusations against us by nailing them to the cross (Col. 2:14), Christ has given us a new nature and a new life, we have been adopted into

God's family, and He calls and empowers us to serve as restored priest-kings in His new creation. They also need to know what this looks like in practical terms. Unfortunately, some of our churches have a long way to go in getting this story across.

And then the narration needs to continue Monday through Saturday:

> Hear, O Israel: The LORD our God, the LORD is one. Love the LORD your God with all your heart and with all your soul and with all your strength. These commandments that I give you today are to be on your hearts. Impress them on your children. Talk about them when you sit at home and when you walk along the road, when you lie down and when you get up. Tie them as symbols on your hands and bind them on your foreheads. Write them on the doorframes of your houses and on your gates.
>
> When the LORD your God brings you into the land he swore to your fathers, to Abraham, Isaac and Jacob, to give you—a land with large, flourishing cities you did not build, houses filled with all kinds of good things you did not provide, wells you did not dig, and vineyards and olive groves you did not plant—then when you eat and are satisfied, be careful that you do not forget the LORD, who brought you out of Egypt, out of the land of slavery.
>
> Fear the LORD your God, serve him only and take your oaths in his name. *Do not follow other gods, the gods of the peoples around you.* (Deut. 6:4–14, emphasis added)

Note in this passage that God's story of change is to be narrated across every facet of our lives. In addition, the passage places a particular emphasis on the need for such narration to take place in the context of economic growth and poverty alleviation! In the passage above, God is leading His people out of the grinding poverty of Egypt and into the prosperity of His kingdom in Canaan. He knows that His people will be tempted to interpret this prosperity through the stories of change of the cultures around them. As Michael Rhodes and Robby Holt explain in *Practicing the King's Economy*:

> *Idolatry is an economic issue.* When we read about the Israelites worshiping the god Baal in 1 Kings 18, we tend to think of them developing a preference for wooden idol images. But the primary attraction to Baal wasn't a pretty statue; it was an economic promise. For the nations around Israel, Baal was the "rider of the clouds," who brought the rains and blessed the earth. When Baal showed up, the heavens rained oil, the rivers ran with honey, mothers gave birth to healthy children, and even the dead could be raised. Little wonder, then, that when King Ahab chose to marry a woman from Baal territory, the farmers in Israel built a house for this new god and welcomed him to the neighborhood (see 1 Kings 16:31).
>
> Of course, most Israelites probably didn't totally reject Yahweh, the God of Israel. They likely continued going to church, paying their tithes, and saying a prayer or two now and again—especially on holidays. They just added Baal worship to their insurance policy. After all, if you're a farmer, it's only practical to invest in getting the rider of the clouds to like you.[8]

The last paragraph is more than speculation. Indeed, God railed on Israel for paying lip service to Him in formal worship but then failing to implement the systems and practices of His kingdom both in how they earned their income and in what they did with it (Isa. 1:10–17; 58:1–10). And as a direct result of this economic idolatry, God sent His holy nation and royal priesthood into captivity.

All of life, including our economic lives, is an act of worship to some god. Hence, separating economic growth and poverty alleviation from worship of God plunges people further into idolatry. Welcome to the American Dream, the same dream that the poverty alleviation movement is bringing to poor people all across the globe.[9]

Aware of the temptation of economic idolatry, God gives Israel a tool to combat this temptation: constant narration of God's story of change as described in the passage from Deuteronomy: *Hey kids, you like these grapes? They are a gift from God, so let's thank Him for His provision. And let's share some with the neighbors, because some pests killed their vines. Hey, we get to plant the new crop of wheat today. Let's ask God to show us the best way to care for the soil and the seeds, because He loves His creation. And let's ask God to bless the wheat, because it won't grow without His sustaining hand.*

With its heavy emphasis on solving our legal problems so that our souls can go to heaven, Evangelical Gnosticism doesn't have the content it needs for such narration. Because it doesn't really see Christ as Lord of all, Evangelical Gnosticism essentially abandons people—both materially poor and non-poor—to false gods and their erroneous stories of change from Monday through Saturday. We don't need any more "Handouts + Evangelism" or any more "Economic Empowerment + Evangelism," as we saw in *Becoming Whole* chapter 4. Rather, we need restoration to wholeness *from God, through God, and for God* (see Rom. 11:36).

Questions for Reflection:

1. What is the story of change that is on your mind as you go throughout your day? What preoccupies your thoughts?

_____

_____

_____

_____

_____

_____

2. How do the various stakeholders (financial supporters, staff, materially poor people) in your ministry define success?

_____

_____

_____

_____

3. How do the various stakeholders (financial supporters, staff, materially poor people) in your ministry believe that success can be achieved?

_____

_____

_____

_____

4. How could your ministry improve its narration of the Bible's goals and way of achieving those goals throughout the day?

_____

_____

_____

_____

Story
Conquering false gods
and erroneous stories
of truth

Ministry Design Principle 5: Integrate God's story of change into technical training

One way to pursue the previous principle is to integrate God's story of change into the technical components of the ministry. For example, most poverty alleviation efforts include some type of training: agricultural training to foster *better* farming practices, hygiene training to lead to *better* sanitation practices, jobs training to develop *better* work habits. There is an implicit story of change in all such training, as "*better*" necessarily involves notions about what the goal is and how this goal can be achieved.

Because the technical features of this training imply a goal and a way of achieving this goal, there is need for the biblical story of change to inform the technical training, thereby combatting the false stories of change from the surrounding culture. Without this biblical perspective, people will tend to *automatically* and *unconsciously* default to the story of change they have absorbed from their surrounding culture. In the Majority World, this means people will combine the new agricultural techniques with visits to the local witch doctor; and if the harvest ends up being bigger, the thank offerings to the gods will be bigger as well. And in the West, it means that people will think that earning a higher income depends solely on their abilities and efforts, and any increases in income will be used to reinforce people's self-centered materialism.

For example, the Chalmers Center's *Plan a Better Business* curriculum is a resource that Majority World churches can use to train groups of materially poor people, including members of the savings and credit associations described in chapter 1. The first lesson asks: *What makes a successful business?* After receiving answers from the participants, the facilitator's script points them to the ultimate goal of God's story of change:

> We all must earn profit from our businesses in order
> to buy food, clothing, and pay school fees for our
> children. True success, however, comes by honoring
> God in our businesses. When we plan our business
> well, we honor God by being good managers of the
> work and resources He has created for us.[10]

As illustrated in Figure 3.1, the lessons also emphasize the proper way to achieve the goal, steering participants away from traditional religion's manipulation of spiritual forces toward reliance upon Jesus Christ. In this lesson, the "diviner" is another term for a witch doctor, the person whom traditional religionists would typically consult to help them manipulate the spirits with amulets and powders. As this lesson demonstrates, participants are encouraged to trust

Jesus Christ to help them in their businesses, for He has power over everything, including spiritual forces.

Figure 3.1
Excerpt from Facilitator's Guide to *Plan a Better Business*

Today we are going to talk about Step 5: Find Help for Your Business.

USE A STORY TO IDENTIFY WAYS TO FIND HELP TO IMPROVE YOUR BUSINESS – 12 MINUTES

When you want to improve or expand your business, sometimes you need extra help to know how to make the proper changes.

Neema's Search for Help with Her Business

Neema wants to make more profit. She fears that her business will not provide enough for school clothes and fees in the coming year. She plans to grow her business by selling stew, kedjenou, and attiéké, plus another product. She begins to look for help to expand her business. She asks a local diviner for help to make the best decision. The man gives her an amulet to hang in her shop and a powder to sprinkle outside the door of her competitor's business.

Turn to a partner and discuss:

> **What similar practices occur in our community?**

Give 2 or 3 participants an opportunity to share. Thank and praise participants.

Troubles certainly come to us all, and we feel desperate and afraid of failure. In these times, God may seem distant, and we are tempted to trust only in our own abilities, or to ask the diviners or spirits for help with our business. However, the Bible says: Open the Scriptures and read Deuteronomy 18:10–13:

> Let no one be found among you who sacrifices their son or daughter in the fire, who practices divination or sorcery, interprets omens, engages in witchcraft, or casts spells, or who is a medium or spiritist or who consults the dead. Anyone who does these things is detestable to the LORD. . . . You must be blameless before the LORD your God.

> **What does this mean for us when we seek help for our businesses?**

Give 2 or 3 participants an opportunity to share. Thank and praise participants.

As the people of God, we are not to consult diviners or follow their advice. When we are part of God's family, we can ask Him in faith to help us. He gives us the power and strength that we need to persevere through difficulties.

Open the Scriptures to 1 John 5:14. The Bible says:

"This is the confidence we have in approaching God: that if we ask anything according to his will, he hears us."

> › **Why does God hear us when we pray to Him?**

When Jesus died on the cross, He gave us this access to God. He conquered all other powers *(Colossians 2:15)*. He died to forgive our mistakes—all of them—even when we look to other sources for help instead of looking to Him.

> › **What questions or comments do you have?**

When working in the US, it is the erroneous stories of change derived from Western Naturalism and Evangelical Gnosticism that must be confronted, both of which see the American Dream as the goal of this life and both of which trust in human ingenuity and material resources alone to achieve this goal. To combat this, *Faith & Finances*, which teaches biblical principles of financial stewardship, emphasizes several things:

- God is not far away. On the contrary, He is actively engaged with His world, including every aspect of our daily lives, working to achieve His goal of making all things new.

- Human beings are not wired to be the individualistic, consuming robots of Western civilization. Rather, we are wired to live in loving community with God, self, others, and the rest of creation.

- God is restoring His people to be a community of image bearers who steward His resources by bringing glory to Him.

- We can call on Jesus Christ to help us as we seek to be restored in our relationships and our finances.

For example, the first lesson states,

> Jesus cares about fixing all parts of our lives . . . restoring us to reflect God's image and glory. Although the

Fall has broken everything, Jesus is repairing and
restoring all things—including our money and relationships. He is not only concerned with the *spiritual*
parts of us, but *all* parts of us—finances included!

As His children, we play a key role in God's work.
No matter how much money we have, we have a special role to play in caring for God's resources. This
is an exciting responsibility—although God didn't
have to, He has chosen to use our money to do His
work in the world. For God's people, our goals in
money management are not just creating wealth
or security but seeking first the kingdom of God in
the world. His kingdom often looks different than
mainstream society. In God's economy, true financial
flourishing always goes hand in hand with restored
community.[11]

The curriculum then illustrates these concepts in scenarios that
are highly relevant to the daily lives of low-income people—dealing with emergencies, avoiding predatory lenders, opening a bank
account, getting out of debt, repairing credit histories, and so on—
showing participants how Christ can empower them to steward their
resources to advance His kingdom. For example, the chapter on
managing debt leads participants through a discussion of Deuteronomy 15:1–11 and then says,

From this passage we can see God's heart for all
people to have enough to care for themselves. His
plan was not for credit to break relationships or to
enslave people. It seems as if God recognizes how
credit can help us in certain situations, but there are
limits—high interest rates should not cause financial
struggle and broken relationships. Credit should
never be used to put another person in bondage.
Remember, God's intention from the beginning has

been to restore our relationships to reflect His image and glory. Our first theme on the wall reminds us that He sent Jesus to accomplish this—to make all things new.[12]

The lesson then goes into the technical aspects of calculating interest, reducing debt, and improving one's credit score, concluding with the following:

> Jesus' sacrifice on the cross gives us freedom from bondage to our sin and hope in the midst of our struggles. Remember, He promises to repair and make all things new! Let's close by asking Him for freedom from the bondage of debt, both for ourselves and our communities.[13]

What is proposed here is quite different from the "Handouts + Evangelism" strategy or the "Economic Empowerment + Evangelism" strategy described in chapter 3 of *Becoming Whole*, strategies which reinforce the message of Evangelical Gnosticism: *Trust Jesus so that your soul will go to heaven when you die, and then chase the American Dream now.* On the contrary, Ministry Design Principle 5 is after whole-person, whole-life discipleship that seeks to help people live as priest-kings in God's kingdom right now.

Consistent with Ministry Design Principle 2, *Faith & Finances* is used in a group, a learning community that typically includes both the materially poor and non-poor. Although the topics are geared toward the former, all the community members benefit from hearing about God's story of change, for people of all income levels need to be freed from the erroneous teachings of Western Naturalism and Evangelical Gnosticism. As the messages of mutual brokenness and Christ's reconciling work set in, the group becomes an arena in which both parties can start to embrace God's story of change: *the goal is not for the materially poor to become like the materially non-poor, but rather for both parties to be conformed to the image of Christ.* And in the process, the bonds within the group become deeper, as both parties realize that they need Christ's reconciling work to become whole. As Matt states, *Faith & Finances* "has created a relational glue that wasn't there in our congregation before."

Of course, no single course can completely combat the lies that people have absorbed from the surrounding culture since birth. Indeed, as Ministry Design Principle 5 states, God's story of change must be narrated throughout life. Matt and Maurice didn't just take a course together and then—*shazam!*—were completely whole. Rather, they have embarked on a lifetime journey of mutual discipleship, "being with" each other as Christ does His work on both of them and uses them to extend His kingdom. But courses like this *can* help to establish a solid foundation for becoming whole, because they can initiate the kinds of communities that we need to thrive as God designed, communities centered on Christ and His life-giving narrative that will last long after the course is over.

Questions for Reflection:

1. What is the implicit story of change in your training and curricula?

   _____

   _____

   _____

   _____

2. How could your training and curricula better combat the false gods and erroneous stories of change in the culture in which your ministry is operating?

   _____

   _____

   _____

   _____

3. What specific actions will you take to improve your ministry's training and curriculum so that they more fully reflect the biblical story of change?

_____

_____

_____

_____

Story

Conquering false gods and erroneous stories of truth

Ministry Design Principle 6: Use funding sources that permit God's story of change to be integrated into technical training

Roughly fifteen years ago, Christian ministry leaders were invited to the Capitol in Washington, DC, to hear a presentation about President George W. Bush's Faith-Based Initiative. The presenter, a very senior member of the administration, was tasked with explaining how Christian ministries could now access federal funds on equal footing with secular nonprofit organizations. From the perspective of many Christians, the Faith-Based Initiative was one of the administration's crowning achievements. The room was filled with excitement as the ministry leaders anticipated being able to receive more funds to expand their work.

The administration official spent two hours carefully describing the various policies and procedures of the brightest jewel in the administration's crown. And then he closed with this: "Despite all that I have just said, my biggest hope is that most of your ministries never apply for a penny of these federal funds. You see, what makes your ministries so special is your ability to share Jesus Christ. If you take this money, I fear it will undermine your effectiveness."[14]

Boom.

The point is *not* that government money is always bad. Indeed, there are many good features of the Faith-Based Initiative, and, depending on the nature of the organization's work, there are sometimes ways to creatively use government funds without undermining the organization's mission. In fact, I once obtained a government grant for a ministry for something that didn't undermine the organization's Christ-centered focus.

But we do need to be extremely careful that our funding sources do not undermine our ability to live according to a biblical story of change, in which the goal and means of achieving the goal are centered on Jesus Christ and His reconciling work *in all aspects of life*. Many sources of funds, including government funds, make this extremely difficult—and in some cases impossible. *Indeed, government funds cannot be used to create or disseminate any of the curricula described in Ministry Design Principle 5.*

Many donors essentially require Evangelical Gnosticism in the design of the ministry: the donor's funds can be used to run the technical features of the program, but any religious teachings need to be separated by time and location from those technical features. And many of God's people say, "No problem! We can use the donor's funds to pay for 'secular' training on microfinance, financial education, jobs preparedness, and so forth, and then we can have separate Bible lessons that teach people how to get their souls saved." This is pure Evangelical Gnosticism! It diminishes the lordship of Christ and ultimately deforms everybody involved in the ministry. Development expert Bryant Myers observes:

> As soon as the [materially poor people] figure out, as
> we in the West have, that technology works without
> God as part of the explanation, God is dropped from
> that explanation. The bottom line is that we need to
> be concerned about who gets worshiped at the end
> of the development program. Jayakumar Christian
> reminds us that whatever we put at the center of the
> program during its lifetime will tend to be what the
> community worships in the end.[15]

Restoration to wholeness is *from God, through God, and for God* (see Rom. 11:36), so removing Him from the center of the ministry is not a recipe for success. Just ask Matt and Maurice.

Worship and Poverty Alleviation

Human beings are transformed into the image of whatever god they worship, so at the core of effective poverty alleviation is worship of the one true God.

Questions for Reflection:

1. Are there any ways that your ministry's sources of funding are undermining its ability to communicate who Jesus Christ really is: the Creator, Sustainer, and Reconciler of all things (Col. 1:15–23)?

2. Who are the ministry's stakeholders (financial supporters, staff, materially poor people) worshiping as a result of your ministry? Who do they believe is responsible for any success that your ministry has?

3. What do you see your stakeholders (financial supporters, staff, materially poor people) becoming like over time? What does this suggest about the god(s) they are worshiping?

CHAPTER FOUR

REPLACING DESTRUCTIVE FORMATIVE PRACTICES (PART 1)

> Whatever you have learned or received or heard from me, or seen in me—put it into practice. And the God of peace will be with you.
> —PHILIPPIANS 4:9

> That's how we measure real development—whenever the people we're serving begin to serve.[1]
> —MARGARET JONES, DIRECTOR OF OPERATIONS FOR AN AFFILIATE OF JOBS FOR LIFE, 2018

I don't want to die anymore. I want to live and tell the world of how Christ has made a difference in my life."

Yes, Cindy once wanted to die. But that was before she encountered Advance Memphis, a Christian organization that ministers in one of the poorest neighborhoods in the country. Advance's mission is "to empower adults in South Memphis to break cycles of unemployment, establish economic stability, reconcile relationships, and restore dignity through knowledge, resources, and skills by the power of Jesus Christ."[2] Toward that end, Advance uses an amazing portfolio of programs to restore people as priest-kings: jobs preparedness training,[3] a staffing agency, financial education,[4] entrepreneurship training,[5] a matched savings program, GED preparation, and addiction recovery. In 2009, Cindy graduated from the Jobs for Life[6] class at Advance Memphis, a biblically based jobs preparedness program that teaches the soft skills of finding and keeping work and that connects participants to potential employers. A year later, Cindy wrote,

> Before I came through the program, my life was a total mess. I lived in chaos, I was sad, I was angry at my family, myself and even God. I didn't understand why God allowed my mother to die when I was 5 years old and put me through such dysfunctional childhood events. I didn't understand why I was trying to find fulfillment in alcohol and drugs. I didn't understand why I couldn't function in everyday society without wanting to die. I had no hope for my future.
>
> When I sat in Jobs for Life class every day, listening to not only the instructors but to my conscience, I began to realize that there was a better way to go about living life. I started pursuing a relationship with Christ and became very passionate about making some changes. I became active in Bible studies and the [Alcoholics Anonymous] program. As my heart started changing, so did my thoughts, as well as my life.
>
> I stand amazed at all God has done in my life just in the last year. I am now 18 months sober and feeling better about myself every day. I am on the staff at Advance Memphis now, helping our course graduates find employment when just last year I sat in the staffing office crying because I was ineligible to work through the staffing service. I have attended budget and credit counseling and I am now responsible with a checking and savings account and being able to make some financial amends. I have my own apartment and I am saving towards buying a car.

I have established a relationship with my children when I never thought they would speak to me again. They inquire about my life with Christ and have occasionally driven across town to attend church with me. I located my youngest son through the internet and now get to spend time with him when he didn't even know me. My sisters and I are communicating and visiting with each other when I hadn't spoken to them in years. My brother calls me "little sis" again. I've had the pleasure of meeting and talking to nieces and nephews for the first time ever. My parents came from Florida to visit with me and God is definitely doing some restoration in our relationships. My dad and I cried together and forgave each other and my stepmom, who I used to hold deep resentment towards, is now becoming one of my best friends. I value relationships today, when I used to cringe at the thought of being open and honest about who I really am.

I am proud of who I am today and all that I have accomplished through Christ. I often pray that God will allow me to share my experience, strength, and hope with others so I can be an encouragement to anybody who is in a hopeless situation. My life has radically changed today. I smile, I laugh, and I enjoy my family and friends. I have a job that I absolutely love with co-workers that don't judge me, and they love me for who I am.[7]

Ten years later, Cindy continues to serve as a program administrator at Advance—a loving community centered on the person of Jesus Christ that fosters *formative practices* that seek to restore priest-kings to worshipful work. This is the kingdom of God bursting forth in the heart of inner-city Memphis, Tennessee.

THE KINGDOM COMMUNITY:
REPLACING DESTRUCTIVE FORMATIVE PRACTICES (PART 1)

Cindy had to forsake destructive ways of living and embrace a new way of life, a new set of practices that are consistent with God's kingdom. In this chapter and the next, we examine *formative practices* that can help all the stakeholders in poverty alleviation ministries live more faithfully into God's kingdom. These practices are *formative* because, in addition to being productive in their own right, they help shape the hearts of the community members—transforming them into different people from who they were before. Just as repeatedly dribbling, passing, and shooting makes a person a better basketball player, so repeatedly acting like priest-kings makes us better priest-kings—and thus we become more whole.[8]

The idea that people's actions shape their hearts is consistent with a biblical understanding of the nature of human beings. The heart, or soul, has three facets: mind, affections, and will (or actions). Hence, the best way to shape a person's heart is not simply to pour more knowledge into his or her brain. Rather, training the heart involves capturing people's imaginations (minds), moving their emotions (affections), and encouraging them to act (wills).[9] Indeed, the Bible teaches that knowledge and practice belong together, for when they are separated, it shows we don't really understand or act rightly:

> Do not merely listen to the word, and so deceive yourselves. Do what it says. Anyone who listens to the word but does not do what it says is like someone who looks at his face in a mirror and, after looking at himself, goes away and immediately forgets what he looks like. (James 1:22–24)

Beliefs shape our actions, but our actions also shape our beliefs. It is not a one-way street.[10] That is why we are to watch our life and beliefs, not picking between them (1 Tim. 4:16). To claim to believe things but have no real regard to live out those beliefs raises questions about what one actually believes in the first place (James 2:14–26). Godly practices can enlarge our hearts even while godly hearts can drive our practices. And the Bible tells us to guard our hearts, because they are the fundamental driver of our lives (Prov. 4:23). Narrating God's story of change throughout our daily lives is a necessary part of such guarding (Ministry Design Principle 4), but because the heart includes the *affections* and the *will* (or actions) in addition to the *mind*, we need to do more than just listen. We need to become *active listeners*: we need to seek to hear, understand, and engage the Word, which includes acting according to its truth. The narration must be acted on if it is to impact the totality of the human heart, the foundation of both people and the communities they create. This doesn't mean we understand or act perfectly—God knows how often we all fall short, again and again. But it does mean we take both doctrine and life, belief and practice, truth and justice seriously. We refuse to choose! When this is done, love and dignity, grace and responsibility, joy and persistence all are affirmed.

Cindy is a great example of a person who acted on the new story of change she was hearing. She didn't just sit through jobs preparedness training, money management classes, and Bible studies. She acted on what she learned. She joined Alcoholics Anonymous, got a job, started saving, and worked on repairing her relationships. These actions moved her in a positive direction, but they also changed her inner being, transforming her into a completely different person. As Cindy explains, "As my heart started changing, so did my thoughts, as well as my life." Human beings are primarily lovers, and we are transformed into the image of whatever we love the most, the thing that we worship above all else.[11] And one of the things that shapes our hearts is the actions we take. Do we want to grow in our love of God, self, others, and the rest of creation? Practicing loving them is part of what shapes our hearts to love them. Actions that live out God's story are *formative practices*: they change who we are deep inside and help us become whole.

None of this should be misconstrued as some sort of works righteousness. Certainly, we are saved by grace through faith alone and are given the Holy Spirit as a "deposit guaranteeing our inheritance" (Eph. 1:14; see also 2:8–9). Because of Christ's death and resurrection, believers dwell in God's house as His children both now and forevermore. We did nothing to earn this status, and there is nothing we can do to lose it. But growing up and becoming mature as new creatures involves a dynamic interplay between God and His beloved children. We cannot grow up apart from the power of Christ and His indwelling Spirit. As Cindy says, everything she has done has been done "through Christ." But the fact that we need God to work in and through us should not move us to passivity. Rather, it should encourage us to take aggressive action because there is hope (Phil. 2:12–13; 3:13–14). The same power that raised Christ from the dead is at work in us, so we can use that power to be who we really are, to live into God's story, to work at becoming whole (Eph. 1:19–20).

Practicing God's story of change means we stop engaging in the destructive formative practices associated with false gods and their erroneous stories of change. For us in the West, this means rejecting the deforming practices of Western Naturalism and Evangelical Gnosticism, both of which see the American Dream as the goal for this life, practices that include:

- acting autonomously, as though God does not exist or is irrelevant

- looking out for number one without regard for others

- earning and consuming as much as possible

- trusting in education, technology, wealth, and power alone

- acting prideful about our wealth or accomplishments

- selfishly competing with others or using them for our own gain

- exploiting God's creation

The American Dream isn't working for us, so we shouldn't impose it on materially poor people. This means that our poverty alleviation ministries should reject practices that elevate the material over the spiritual and relational dimensions of reality, that trust in technology and material resources alone to overcome poverty, and that see ever-increasing levels of consumption as the goal for this life. In other words, it means moving away from the practices that Evangelical Gnosticism uses to help materially poor people: (1) *Handouts + Evangelism* or (2) *Economic Empowerment + Evangelism.*[12]

Instead, we must pursue practices that treat all the stakeholders as a community of broken-but-restored priest-kings, people who are using the power of Christ's death and resurrection to jointly steward their wide range of gifts to advance His kingdom. This is what it means to improvise the story of God's kingdom, the only story that is fully true. Let's consider some principles that can help us practice this new script together.

Practices
Replacing destructive
formative practices

Ministry Design Principle 7: All the stakeholders should treat each other as members of a community that is jointly stewarding the King's gifts to advance His kingdom.

We have summarized the various stakeholders in a poverty alleviation ministry into three groups: the donors, the ministry employees, and the materially poor people. These stakeholders typically have very different educational, professional, socioeconomic, and cultural backgrounds that can make it difficult for them to even understand each other, much less collaborate. And to make matters worse, these stakeholders have often unconsciously internalized very different stories of change that they have not articulated to themselves, much less to one another. Satan loves to exploit these differences, sowing seeds of distrust within the household of faith and undermining the advancement of Christ's kingdom. This will take some unpacking.

Many donors are businesspeople or have at least worked in the forprofit sector, a world that emphasizes efficiency, productivity, metrics, accountability, rationality, and technological mastery. Because donors have been financially successful, they are typically heroes in their cultures: they are the successful ones; they have won the game of life. So when these brothers and sisters enter the space of poverty alleviation, they tend to enter with confidence and optimism, expecting to experience the same success in this space that they have experienced in the for-profit sector. And they tend to automatically assume that the same organizational model that operates in the for-profit world, or some facsimile thereof, should be used in the ministry world—the profit-making business.

Materially poor people might as well be living on different planets from the donors. They often feel unable to control their individual lives, much less their environments. Technological mastery of the natural world? They'd prefer something to control demons. Getting an advanced degree to climb the corporate ladder? They'd be happy if their kids' teachers would just show up to school every day. And in contrast to the cultural affirmation that donors are accustomed to, the message to the materially poor is that they are inferior, unintelligent, and unwanted; they are the losers in the game of life. So, when these materially poor brothers and sisters learn about a new poverty alleviation ministry, they tend to be pessimistic about the chances that it will work for people like them.

In between these two groups are the ministry staff. Their educational backgrounds and professional experiences tend to be in social work, psychology, health care, teaching, missions, theology, and community development, all of which tend to have a more relational approach to life than the business world. Indeed, the personality profiles of many ministry staff are often at opposite ends of the spectrum from that of their largest financial supporters. While the ministry staff typically do not receive the same social accolades as wealthy donors, they are at least respected by the larger culture for their technical expertise and "sacrificial service."

The space of poverty alleviation entails a collision between these three very different groups of people. How can these differences be managed?

The business world has an answer: The for-profit business enterprise aligns the different backgrounds and interests of investors (donors), the business (ministry), and customers (materially poor people). As pictured in Figure 4.1, in the business world, investors put money into the business, expecting a financial return. The business uses that money and other resources to produce goods and services that the customers want, receiving money from those customers in return. The revenues from the customers are used to pay the employees and to reward the investors. In this world, it doesn't matter that the investors, employees, and customers are all very different from one another, because the business model creates alignment between these different parties. Customers get what they want: goods and services. The employees get what they want: jobs that pay them an income. And the investors get what they want: a financial return on their investment.

FIGURE 4.1

Alignment in the Business Model

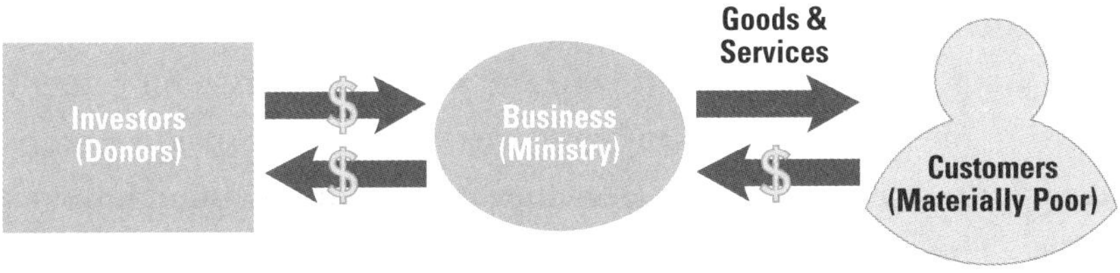

While there are very important lessons that can be gleaned from the business model, the model breaks down in many respects in the nonprofit space. Because the customer (the materially poor person) is typically not paying for the vast majority of goods and services they receive from the poverty alleviation ministry, there is nothing to guarantee that the ministry will actually provide them with what they want at a high quality. Indeed, the financial incentives are for the ministry to serve its donors, because they are the ones who are paying for the employees to have jobs. Hence, while the customer is king in the business sector, in the nonprofit sector the temptation is for the donor to become king, because they are the ones who are paying the bills. In essence, the donor becomes the primary customer. As a result, what donors believe materially poor people need is what materially poor people are going to get. And in the process, the donors' story of change—whether it be Western Naturalism, Evangelical Gnosticism, or something else—gets imposed onto materially poor people.

This problem is exacerbated in the context of church-based ministry, because the church is simultaneously both the ministry and the donor. For example, think of a short-term missions trip. Those going on the trip are the "ministry," but they are also the ones paying for the ministry (along with their friends and relatives). In business terms, we would say that the employees have become the customers! And because the customers are kings, what they want is what poor people are going to get. If the short-term team believes that materially poor people in Tibet need Frisbees, then Frisbees it is!

What to do?

To solve these alignment and incentive problems, many donors, businesspeople, and nonprofit leaders are trying to bring principles from the business world into the nonprofit space. In particular, the exploding social entrepreneurship and social innovation movement is giving birth to a host of new and creative ways to provide materially poor people with the services they really want on a much larger scale.[13] This movement has much to teach us, for it has tremendous insights.

That said, we need to keep God's story of change at the center: the triune God and His people are dwelling in community with one another. These people have already been restored, but are also still being restored as priest-kings (the "now" and "not yet" truth we discussed in *Becoming Whole* chapter 8). As such, all the people in this community—including donors, ministry staff, and materially poor people—are called and empowered to use their gifts, not to seek their own interests, and to advance Christ's kingdom together. Hence, while Figure 4.1 and its translations into the nonprofit sector have some important insights, at the end of the day, Figure 4.2 is the one that should be at the forefront of our minds.

You see, while Advance Memphis' ministry has helped Cindy, she ultimately isn't a "customer" or a program "beneficiary." Instead, she is a coproducer in Christ's kingdom, a restored priest-king who is using her gifts to extend the reign and worship of God and to serve others. No, Cindy wasn't like that the first day she walked into Advance Memphis' offices, because she was still in captivity to the kingdom of darkness. At one time, we all were in such captivity. But through the power of Christ's death and resurrection, she has been set free from bondage and brought into the kingdom of light. And this freedom looks different from pursuing the American Dream. It looks like Cindy, a person who is using her gifts and talents to do the work that God prepared in advance for her to do (Eph. 2:1–10).

FIGURE 4.2

Alignment in the Kingdom Community

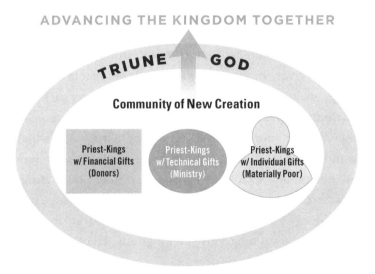

ADVANCING THE KINGDOM TOGETHER

TRIUNE GOD

Community of New Creation

Priest-Kings
w/ Financial Gifts
(Donors)

Priest-Kings
w/ Technical Gifts
(Ministry)

Priest-Kings
w/ Individual Gifts
(Materially Poor)

How can we better practice this kingdom community in the space of poverty alleviation? Clearly, the challenges are enormous. In addition to being quite different from one another, donors, ministries, and materially poor people often live thousands of miles apart. It sure doesn't feel like much of a community, and sadly, it often doesn't function like one. But here are some ways that we can consider improvising together, starting with repentance.

One favorite mantra of many ministry staff is that donors should "pay, pray, and get out of the way." This horrendous attitude reflects the common perspective that staff are the ones with all the expertise and that donors have nothing to contribute besides their money. Further, it fails to recognize that donors are stewarding God's resources and need information to be able to steward it well. Finally, it reduces mind-affections-will-body-relational creatures to human ATM machines. This doesn't love donors' whole being—it doesn't love *them*—and it is an affront to their Creator.

Donors need what all of us need: to use their entire beings to serve as priest-kings; they too want to become whole. For some donors, this involves more than writing checks, for they often have nonfinancial gifts to offer their King. In particular, many donors know a lot about running organizations, which is generally not the strength of most nonprofit ministries. I can attest from personal experience that if God had not brought a number of businesspeople into our lives, the Chalmers Center would probably no longer exist. In addition to giving money, these brothers and sisters have brought leadership, strategic insight, wise counsel, managerial know-how, spiritual mentoring, and deep friendship.

Hence, it's time for ministries to stop stiff-arming practices that keep donors at bay: hiding information, talking about successes but not failures, being closed to advice, avoiding penetrating questions—the list could go on. And ministries need to adopt practices that treat donors like complete human beings, priest-kings who are full partners in advancing Christ's kingdom. Here are a few suggested practices for ministries:

- Stop using the term *donors*, because it reinforces both the human-ATM concept and a giver-receiver dynamic. Consider using alternative terms such as *ministry partners* or *financial resource partners*.

- Be completely transparent in all communications. Financial resource partners are stewarding God's money—which is holy—and they need information to be able to steward it well.

- Be humble enough to learn from your financial resource partners. Ask them questions. Seek their advice. They know things you don't know.

- Look for nonfinancial gifts in your financial resource partners, and give them an opportunity to use those gifts where appropriate.

- Include some financial resource partners on the board, for they are stakeholders in the ministry and often are exceptionally gifted at governance.

- Try to remember that your ministry is only one of thousands of ministries that God is using to advance His kingdom. Those other ministries are not your competitors; they too are members of the new-creation community and are part of your family. Hence, if God has called a financial resource partner to use their gifts to be involved in X and your ministry does Y, help them connect with a ministry that does X. For more on this important topic, see the book by Peter Greer and Chris Horst with Jill Heisey: *Rooting for Rivals: How Collaboration and Generosity Increase the Impact of Leaders, Charities, and Churches.*

- Have the courage to love financial resource partners as whole people. Pray for them, share personal weaknesses with them, and fearlessly speak hard truths into their lives as you would for any brother or sister.

Ministries need to treat materially poor people as partners in kingdom advancement as well.

Part of the reason this sounds strange to us is we have been deformed by the erroneous teachings of Western Naturalism and Evangelical Gnosticism, both of which elevate material gifts over spiritual and relational ones. It's easy to see what financial resource partners bring to the table, but what do the sickly, the homeless, the disabled, and the addicts bring? With a little help, they can bring a ton. Consider the fifty HIV/AIDS sufferers in Kenya, Maurice the formerly homeless man, Joy the educationally challenged, and Cindy the recovering addict. Each of these restored priest-kings is using their gifts to minister in ways that neither financial resource partners nor the rest of us could do. For example, few—if any—missionaries could even meet, much less minister to, the thousand people that the HIV/AIDS sufferers are reaching in rural Kenya. And who is better able to understand what it's like to be homeless in downtown Atlanta than a person who was homeless there? Poverty alleviation is about unlocking these hidden treasures, this gold mine of nonfinancial resources, in joint service to our King. Since most of this book is about how to do this, we will add just a few tips here:

- Stop referring to people who are materially poor with terms like *program "beneficiaries."* Consider alternative language like *participants, friends,* or *partners.* Of course, if they are believers, *brothers and sisters* could work as well.

- Look for ways to include the program participants in the design, execution, and evaluation of the ministry. And, depending on their gifts and readiness, give them opportunities to serve as volunteers, staff, and even board members. Remember, the participants are joint stakeholders in the ministry, not beneficiaries.

- Ensure all the stakeholders are contributing something to the poverty alleviation initiative. Often, financially well-resourced churches partner with churches and ministries that have fewer financial resources. All the partners need to have "skin in the game," including the materially poor participants in the ministry, for all the stakeholders are priest-kings who have gifts they are called to steward.

Of course, while financial resource partners bring many gifts, they have their own limitations and imperfections as well. The fact that somebody knows how to make money selling widgets in Omaha doesn't mean they know how to solve poverty in Zambia. As mind-affections-will-body-relational creatures, materially poor people simply aren't wired like widgets, so they don't respond in the same way. Financial resource partners need to recognize that their expertise in one sector doesn't necessarily translate to the poverty alleviation space.

Similarly, knowing how to run a business doesn't mean one knows everything about running a nonprofit ministry. A nonprofit is a very different sort of animal from a business in terms of culture, staff, incentives, revenue streams, and metrics. Financial resource partners need to be sensitive to these differences and humble enough to listen and learn.

Finally, financial resource partners need to avoid their tendency to see money as the answer to every problem, a tendency that is rooted in the erroneous stories of change of Western Naturalism and Evangelical Gnosticism. Because poverty is rooted in broken relationships that ultimately only Jesus Christ can heal, money simply cannot solve poverty. Yes, money is an extremely important resource for covering the costs of the ministry, but money is not the only resource needed in the fight against poverty. Both the staff and the materially poor participants have gifts to bring to the table, gifts that are every bit as important—if not more so—than the financial gifts. Moreover, some of the stakeholders, especially the materially poor participants, are taking far greater risks than the financial resource partners are. The contributions and sacrifices of all the partners need to be appreciated.

Here are a few suggested practices for financial resource partners:

- Remember that you are stewarding God's money. It's all His.

- Regularly communicate to staff and to materially poor people that they are your partners in ministry who are stewarding gifts that are absolutely essential and that you do not have. Tell them that their gifts, sacrifices, and risks are at least as important as yours, and show them that you really mean it by words and deeds that honor their contributions.

- Respect the time of your ministry partners. They are extremely busy serving *both* materially poor people and you.

- Don't ask to do things that you are not particularly gifted at doing. You are probably not the best person to be doing front-line training of materially poor people in Burkina Faso. God's people in Burkina can do this better than you can. But ministries will have a hard time saying "no" to you. Be humble enough to know where you are gifted, and where you are not.

- Be a humble learner. Ask the staff and materially poor people questions to better understand their worlds, and ask them for suggested readings so you can learn more. They know things you don't know.

- Be transparent and clear in your communications. Too often, ministries are kept guessing: *What does the financial resource partner like? What don't they like? Are they planning to give? If so, how much? When?* Financial resource partners necessarily must be somewhat guarded to protect themselves from the never-ending avalanche of funding requests. But as trust is developed over time with their ministry partners, the lines of communication should become more open as well. It is extremely helpful for the ministry's planning if it knows what the financial resource partner is planning to contribute and when.

- Do whatever you can to stop the "dating" process. Ministries often feel like they need to "wine and dine" financial resource partners, trying to guess when it is appropriate to "pop the question." Financial resource partners can exacerbate the problem, "stringing ministries along" by not being clear in their intentions or by making it difficult to be asked for money. All this wastes enormous amounts of kingdom time, energy, and resources. Financial resource partners should treat ministries like what they are: joint stewards of God's resources. Let's all bring our gifts to our King and move forward together.

There is so much more that needs to be said on this topic. (A good place to start is the book by Rob Martin: *When Money Goes on Mission: Fundraising and Giving in the 21st Century*.) And so much more needs to be done in order for financial resource partners, ministries, and materially poor participants to become better aligned and to become mutually accountable to one another. But an important first step is for all the stakeholders to agree on the story of change, which is one of the primary motivations for *Becoming Whole* and this *Field Guide*.

Questions for Reflection:

1. What specific actions will you take to help all the ministry's stakeholders (financial supporters, staff, materially poor people) to better appreciate one another's different gifts and contributions?

2. What will you do to change the language that the various stakeholders use to refer to one another so you can create a greater sense of community?

3. What other things can you think of that would help the various stakeholders to better link arms in order to serve as a community of restored priest-kings? Be creative.

_____

_____

_____

_____

Practices
Replacing destructive
formative practices

Ministry Design Principle 8: The ministry's marketing and communications should use images and messages that communicate God's story of change.

"Your $25 can save a life, so make your pledge now by calling this number . . ."

Really? $25 is all it takes to overcome false gods and erroneous stories of change, demonic forces, destructive formative practices, broken systems at both the community and macro levels, and broken individuals?

We understand the need for marketing. But part of living faithfully into God's story of change is to communicate truth, and much of the marketing that is going on perpetuates the erroneous ideas of Western Naturalism and Evangelical Gnosticism:

- Money and technology can solve all problems.

- Everything has a quick fix. Just download the app and—*poof*—poverty is solved!

- The poor are helpless and need white Westerners to save them.

We simply don't need any more pictures of Americans drilling a well while a dozen African villagers cheer them on. Yes, this type of marketing might help the ministry raise money, but it is wrong on so many levels:

- It misrepresents what effective poverty alleviation is really all about: highly relational empowerment, not dispensing technology.

- It is demeaning to materially poor people.

- It lauds the wrong heroes.

- It exacerbates the god-complexes of Westerners.

- It is damaging to organizations that are using effective and sustainable approaches by making it more difficult for them to raise money for their work.

The last point really needs to be highlighted. When financial resource partners have been told repeatedly, "For $25 you can buy X (some material item), and X will save a person from poverty," it makes it much harder to raise money for the things that are essential to real poverty alleviation but far less tangible: relationship building, training, community organizing, capacity building, worldview transformation, identifying local assets, leadership development, and more. We need marketing messages that tell the truth about the complexity of poverty and what it really takes to address it.

And we need photos that picture God's story of change. What does this story look like? We are not experts on marketing, so others will need to take up this task. But consider the photos in Figure 4.3. The first photo shows what an effective intervention looks like: a local church leader engaging other local church leaders in a training process about how to identify and mobilize local assets. No, it's not as exciting as pictures of white Americans shoveling grain out the back of trucks, but it's what long-term, sustainable poverty alleviation actually looks like. And the second photo shows what success looks like (*worship*) and gives credit to the right hero for achieving this success (*the triune God*).

FIGURE 4.3

Pictures that Reflect God's Story of Change

Photos courtesy of Ryan Estes.

One of the chief goals of the Christian life is to make God famous, so let's market and communicate His story of change, and His alone.

Questions for Reflection:

1. Take some time to review your ministry's website and other marketing and communications materials. What is the implicit story of change that your ministry is communicating?

_____

_____

_____

_____

2. Who is the hero in your marketing and communications materials?

_____

_____

_____

_____

3. Are materially poor people depicted as pathetic and helpless or as image bearers of the triune God?

_____

_____

_____

_____

Practices

Replacing destructive formative practices

Ministry Design Principle 9: Learn from existing "best practices."

Because Jesus Christ is actively sustaining the entire creation—and because Flatland has never been real— there is good all around us. In particular, despite the fall, God enables both believers and unbelievers to use their God-given abilities to take care of and to develop His creation. In this light, living faithfully as a member of God's kingdom includes stewarding well what He has already enabled others to discover about His kingdom. Indeed, to fail to learn from others is to squander God's gifts. Unfortunately, God's people do this all the time.

Consider, for example, the savings and credit association that Crossroads Church helped the fifty HIV/AIDS sufferers to operate. This savings and credit association reflects "best practices," the term for a methodology that is generally accepted as being superior to other methodologies. Crossroads took the time to learn these best practices before starting its microfinance ministry. Unfortunately, this is not always the case. For years, churches, missionaries, and Christian ministries have plunged headlong into microfinance, using approaches that—in addition to being sub-optimal—are highly likely to do harm to the organization, to materially poor people, and to the name of Christ. There is no excuse for this! Best-practice information is widely available, and even a little bit of time spent doing research could have prevented these problems.

Similarly, there is an explosion of after-school tutoring programs in the US. How many churches and parachurch ministries have taken the time to find out the existing research about best practices in this field? With the availability of the internet, such research is at our fingertips. All we have to do is type "best practices after-school tutoring" or "research after-school tutoring" into any search engine, and a host of resources appear on our screen. Moreover, there are Christian professors, researchers, and practitioners all over the country—they might even be sitting next to us in the pew—whom we could ask for advice. We don't need to reinvent the wheel each time, for others have already figured things out.

Note that we said "learn from," which is not the same as saying "mindlessly adopt." Remember, what a culture considers to be "best" reflects that culture's understanding of what the goal is—its story of change. So, what works best for helping people to achieve the American Dream might not be what works best for helping people to become priest-kings. Different stories of change imply different sets of "best practices." So, there are times when we can simply use what the larger culture has created, and there are times when we will need to modify them or even reject them altogether.[14]

In the space of poverty alleviation, it often is the case that exist-ing best-practice interventions can be modified to fit God's story of change. For example, many of the ministries described in this book use practices that are consistent with best practices in the wider cul-ture, but the Ministry Design Principles have been used to adapt these best practices to be more consistent with God's story of change: rooting the ministry in the church, using supportive groups, inte-grating biblical messages into technical content, praying without ceasing, and so on.

In summary, we have much to learn from our friends in the larger poverty alleviation industry. It is simply sinful to ignore their contri-butions and insights. But the process of becoming whole also looks different from standard approaches to poverty alleviation, and our ministries need to reflect this difference.

Questions for Reflection:

1. Does your ministry reflect best practices, appropriately adjusted to be consistent with the biblical story of change?

2. If you're unsure or if the answer is "no," what does that indi-cate about your ministry's goals and ways of achieving those goals?

3. Does your ministry have the attitude of a humble learner, or does it function as if it is the only source of knowledge?

_____

_____

_____

_____

4. What will you do to ensure that your ministry can be a better learner?

_____

_____

_____

_____

CHAPTER FIVE

REPLACING DESTRUCTIVE FORMATIVE PRACTICES (PART 2)

I never thought I could do all of this. If you love the Lord, you should help others achieve things they can't even dream of. God wants us to use our time, talents, and finances to cause dreams to happen.[1]
—DONALD JENKINS, GRADUATE OF ADVANCE MEMPHIS' *WORK LIFE* TRAINING, 2014

The crucible of our formation is in the monotony of our daily routines.[2]
—TISH HARRISON WARREN, AUTHOR, 2017

About a year ago, I (Brian) went for one of my regular evening walks through the neighborhood. My nerves were shot, and I was exhausted. I had been working too hard on too many things for far too long. In particular, writing about becoming whole was, well, making me less whole. I hoped some exercise would clear my head, so I plugged in my earbuds and headed out the door.

After a few blocks, I ran into Bob, a fellow I've known casually for several years. I didn't really feel like talking, but it was clear that he did, so I reluctantly pulled out my earbuds. I'm better at writing about relationships than I am at actually having them.

As we talked, Bob confided that he had become homeless and wondered whether I could help him. I started to explain that I wasn't in a position to help because I was writing a book on how to help poor people and didn't have the time. But fearing that God might strike me dead on the spot for my unparalleled level of hypocrisy, I called home to my wife and asked whether Bob could sleep on our couch that night. Knowing that Jill was overwhelmed with her own work, I was hoping she would say no so I could tell both Bob and God that it was her fault that we couldn't help. Adam once tried blaming Eve, and it didn't work out too well, but I was willing to give it a shot.

Of course, my loving wife said yes, and Bob ended up living with us for about three weeks, becoming a family friend in the process. We have continued to walk with Bob through a host of ups and downs for the past year. In fact, as I write this, he texts me, as he does throughout the day, every day. It's not always clear where Bob's life is heading, but one thing is certain: the fact that I was so far behind on writing my portions of this book was his fault! Yes, I'm pretty good at blame shifting.

As we got to know Bob better, we learned that he had been living in his car for over a year and had been struggling for decades. A host of external and internal factors over the course of Bob's life have contributed to his situation, none of which are easy to fix. Due to an affordable housing shortage in our city, there simply aren't many places available for him to live. And even if he can find a place, the amount of financial assistance that he receives from the government is not sufficient to pay the rent. So, Bob needs to work at least part-time. This is easier said than done, because in addition to the challenge of finding a job, Bob is hampered by physical and mental health issues, which need more professional attention that is not free. There are numerous obstacles to ending Bob's homelessness, and even more to his becoming whole.

THE KINGDOM COMMUNITY: REPLACING DESTRUCTIVE FORMATIVE PRACTICES (PART 2)

This chapter continues the discussion from the last chapter, examining *formative practices* that are consistent with God's kingdom in the space of poverty alleviation.[3]

Practices

Replacing destructive
formative practices

Ministry Design Principle 10: Use relief, rehabilitation, and development appropriately.

As we approached several area churches looking for help for Bob, we found that most of them had benevolence funds that were set up to offer immediate assistance, such as providing clothes or paying for him to stay in a motel for a week. There is often a need for this type of assistance, but such help is a "drop in a bucket" compared to what it will really take to restore Bob.

You see, different kinds of material poverty abound, even though they often look the same on the surface. There is a huge difference between the material poverty of a well-functioning family whose house is suddenly wiped out by a tornado and a homeless person who has been struggling with a host of external and internal issues for many years. On the surface they look the same: both are lacking housing. But the underlying circumstances that have contributed to their plight are very different and require entirely different responses.

In this light, as pictured in Figure 5.1, it is helpful to think of three broad categories of poverty alleviation:

FIGURE 5.1

Relief, Rehabilitation, and Development

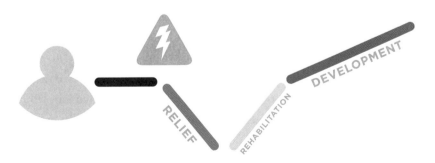

Adapted from Steve Corbett and Brian Fikkert, *When Helping Hurts: How to Alleviate Poverty without Hurting the Poor . . . and Yourself*, 2nd ed., Fig. 4.1 (Chicago: Moody Publishers, 2012), 100.

- *Relief* can be defined as the urgent and temporary provision of emergency aid to reduce immediate suffering from a natural or man-made crisis. After a crisis, there is a need to halt the free fall and to "stop the bleeding," and this is what relief attempts to do. The key feature of relief is a provider-receiver dynamic in which the provider gives assistance—often material—to the receiver. Because the individual or community is in a crisis, they are typically asked to contribute little or nothing toward reducing their own suffering. Though not the point of the passage, the Good Samaritan's bandaging of the helpless man who lay bleeding along the roadside is an excellent example of relief applied appropriately (Luke 10:29–37).

- *Rehabilitation* begins as soon as the bleeding stops, and it seeks to restore people to the positive elements of their pre-crisis conditions. Because the individual or community is no longer helpless, the key feature of rehabilitation is a dynamic of working *with* the people, asking them to take positive actions as they participate in their own recovery.

- *Development* is a process of ongoing change that moves all the people involved—both the materially poor and materially non-poor—closer to being in right relationship with God, self, others, and the rest of creation than they have been in the past. For materially poor people who are able-bodied, development includes their moving toward fulfilling their calling of glorifying God by working to support their families and to share with their neighbors the fruits of that work. The key dynamic in development is promoting an empowering process in which all the people involved—both the "helpers" and the "helped"—become more of what God created them to be. Development is not done *to* people or *for* people but *with* people.

If an individual or community is in a crisis resulting from an unexpected large bill, a physical assault, a medical emergency, a natural disaster, or a civil war, then relief is the appropriate response. In these cases, we need to help people quickly and sufficiently in order to stabilize the chaos created by the crisis. Although people sometimes need relief repeatedly, it is most often appropriate only for people experiencing a one-time crisis.

But the vast majority of materially poor people in the world are not experiencing a one-time crisis. Rather, they are battling a chronic state of poverty created by a complex set of forces. While they may not be able to change all the factors contributing to their situation, if they can contribute *something* to improve their circumstances, then development—not relief—is the proper approach (see Figure 5.2). It is profoundly important to note that when using a developmental approach, it might be helpful for the ministry to provide money or other material resources to the low-income person it is assisting, but this should be done in a way that builds upon the gifts and resources that the person is also contributing to their own progress, for the goal is to restore them as priest-kings, not reduce them to beggars.

FIGURE 5.2

Development is the Right Approach for Most Poverty

Adapted from Steve Corbett and Brian Fikkert, *When Helping Hurts: How to Alleviate Poverty without Hurting the Poor... and Yourself,* 2nd ed., Fig. 4.1 (Chicago: Moody Publishers, 2012), 100.

Relief doesn't ask people to take actions to improve their situation; development does. Relief is done *to* people or *for* people; development is done *with* people.

Relief says to the family in which the forty-year-old father has had a stroke, "Yes, of course we will help you financially until you get back on your feet."

Development says to the person repeatedly asking for help in paying their electric bill, "Yes, we can help you, but only if you are open to exploring with us the reasons you are struggling to pay your bill and to doing what is needed to avoid this problem in the future. Can we help you make some necessary changes in your life?"

One of the most common and detrimental mistakes that poverty alleviation ministries make is using a relief approach when the situation calls for development. Because we have been so heavily influenced by Western Naturalism and Evangelical Gnosticism, we tend to see life—including material poverty—in material terms. Hence, we view poverty as being about a lack of material things and give repeated handouts of shoes, clothing, food, or money to people who are not helpless and who are not in a crisis. This approach can deepen the very feelings of shame and inadequacy that are often the root causes of material poverty. In addition, giving handouts, especially repeatedly, can foster a mindset of dependency or entitlement, undermining people's capacity and drive to support themselves and their families through their own work.

Of course, knowing exactly when to use relief, rehabilitation, and development is not always clear, for there are all sorts of added complexities in the real world.

For example, your ministry is not the only option in town. So, even if you believe you are only giving financial assistance "just this one time," the other ministries in your community may be doing the same. As a result, your "one-time" gift may actually be just one of a long series of handouts that collectively are enabling a person to persist in chronic poverty. If a person is able-bodied and not in a serious crisis, a ministry should be quick to use creative ways to walk with the person as he or she takes actions to contribute to their own improvement (development) and slow to simply give them material resources (relief).

Another complexity is that communities and the individuals within those communities might need different approaches. For example, a community struggling with chronic poverty might need development overall, but some of the individuals or families within that community might need relief because they are suffering from a real crisis and legitimately need immediate aid.

On top of this is the additional complexity that the same individual might repeatedly move back and forth between needing relief and development. For example, New Hope Church was pursuing a developmental approach with Sarah, a single mother of three who was living in a housing project. New Hope was providing spiritual counsel and discipleship to Sarah, helping her to find work and assisting her with transportation and child care. Progress was slow, but Sarah was trying to overcome some of the behavioral issues that had contributed to her material poverty. One day, as Sarah was walking home from the store, she was mugged by two men who stole the bags of groceries she had been carrying. The church wisely discerned that while Sarah generally needed development, she also suddenly needed relief. This was not a time to place all sorts of conditions on Sarah before she could get assistance. Sarah and her kids were in a crisis and needed help, so the church bought her several bags of groceries to replace what had been stolen.

Finally, at least on the surface, not all low-income people fit the description that we have been using throughout this book: people with a marred identity who are struggling with a sense of shame or inferiority. Indeed, like many of us, some low-income people wrestle with pride and an unwillingness to submit to authority. As always, you will need to adjust the general principles in this book to the particular nature of the people with whom you are walking.

In light of this complexity, there is a general rule of thumb that can be helpful: *avoid paternalism, habitually doing things for people that they can do for themselves.*[4] Paternalism comes in a variety of forms:

- **Resource Paternalism:** giving people resources that they do not truly need and/or could acquire on their own

- **Spiritual Paternalism:** taking spiritual leadership away from the materially poor, assuming we have more to offer than they do

- **Knowledge Paternalism:** assuming we have all the best ideas about how to do things

- **Labor Paternalism:** doing work for the materially poor that they can do for themselves

- **Managerial Paternalism:** taking ownership of change away from the materially poor, insisting that they follow our "better, more efficient" way of doing things

Although paternalism is a problem in every setting, it is particularly tempting for Westerners working in the Majority World. The gap between our standard of living and that of materially poor people in such settings is so dramatic that it is difficult not to rush in with all sorts of resources and take over. Alvin Mbola, a Kenyan community development worker who serves in Kibera, the sprawling slum on the outskirts of Nairobi, describes the situation as follows:

> To many people, the Kibera slum in Nairobi, Kenya, is a place with no equals. It is filthy, congested, degraded, and unfit for human habitation. Like the proverbial scriptural reference to the birthplace of Jesus Christ, many people believe that "nothing good can come out of Kibera." Therefore, most remedies directed toward Kibera are motivated by the sympathy of outsiders, who often give handouts in an attempt to cushion the residents against their perceived, gigantic problems.

In reality, many of the problems of Kibera stem from chronic issues that can only be solved through a consistent and long-term relationship between the change agent and the residents. Changes within individuals and communities are not instantaneous; long-term relationships are needed to bring out the best of "what is" and of "what could be." The people in Kibera have capacities, skills, and resources that need to be tapped if genuine development is to be realized, but the process of identifying and mobilizing these gifts and assets takes time.

Unfortunately, for many years non-government organizations working in Kibera have tended to operate on the basis of "quick fixes." Frustrations set in because changes in individuals are not coming as quickly as anticipated. Many of these organizations then either close down or move to other parts of the country, leaving people in a worse situation than they were before.

It appears that many donors are willing to give to any venture as long as they see pictures of "dilapi-dated" Kibera. . . .

Of course, there are some occasions in which there is a need for relief work in Kibera. For example, oftentimes there are fire breakouts where houses and business premises are gutted down. It might be necessary to bring in outside resources to provide relief and to rehabilitate these homes and businesses. But even in these situations, caution should be taken so that the relief efforts are not prolonged to the point in which they undermine local people's stewardship of their own lives and communities.

The root issue in all of these considerations is that God, who is a worker, ordained work so that humans could worship Him through their work. Relief efforts applied inappropriately often cause the beneficiaries to abstain from work, thereby limiting their relation-ship with God through distorted worship or through no worship at all.[5]

Relief applied inappropriately undermines the development of priest-kings and runs counter to God's story of change.

That said, don't get twisted in knots and paralyzed by trying to categorize people into relief, rehabilitation, or development. When faced with a decision, ask yourself the following question: *If I take this action, will I contribute to or detract from the long-term goal of empowering this person to serve as a priest-king, living in right relationship with God, self, others, and the rest of creation?* Ask the Holy Spirit for wisdom and discernment, and then move forward humbly but without fear. Jesus Christ is actively present, and He will accomplish His purposes despite our mistakes. All we can do is our best.

The problem for Bob—and for many materially poor people around the world—is that churches and ministries are generally providing relief when development is what is needed most. This reality is tragically ironic, for development is essentially just holistic discipleship, which is at the very heart of the Great Commission! No doubt, development is more difficult than relief, but as the examples in this *Field Guide* illustrate, churches and parachurch ministries are effectively using developmental approaches all over the world; savings and credit associations, circles of support, jobs preparedness training, and financial education are all developmental approaches. And note that many of these are tiny and extremely poor churches ministering in the poorest countries of the Majority World. Poverty alleviation isn't fundamentally about money; it's about reconciling relationships through the power of Christ's death and resurrection. And King Jesus is present and available to His people, whether they are rich or poor, because they are united to Him.

Bob doesn't need help for just a week; he needs help for years. But such help should not entail a never-ending series of handouts.

Rather, it should take a developmental approach: a team of people walking with Bob across time, providing support, encouragement, and accountability as he uses his gifts to move ahead. This could include offering various forms of material assistance, for Bob needs help with rent for more than just a week. But it mostly involves identifying, strengthening, and mobilizing Bob's gifts and increasingly asking him to steward those gifts to the glory of God, for this is the essence of being a priest-king.

Questions for Reflection:

1. Is your ministry simply providing handouts to able-bodied people over long periods of time?

_____

_____

_____

2. Are there any ways in which your ministry is being paternalistic? Be specific.

_____

_____

_____

3. Do you see any evidence that your ministry has created unhealthy dependencies? How has it done so?

_____

_____

_____

4. What specific things will your ministry do to move away from doing things *to* or *for* people to doing things *with* people?

_____

_____

_____

_____

Practices
Replacing destructive
formative practices

Ministry Design Principle 11: Start by focusing on assets, not needs.

When thinking about helping a materially poor individual or community, what enters your mind first? Many of us focus on what is lacking in terms of resources. As a result, we then pursue a "needs-based" approach, focusing on deficits and needs, and assuming that the individual or community has little to offer to combat their problems. With a needs-based approach, the assumption is that the resources, solutions, and initiative will not come primarily from the materially poor people but from the ministry. A needs-based approach often exacerbates the very dynamic that we need to get out of in poverty alleviation: people with god-complexes handing out material resources to people with marred identities.

In contrast, an "asset-based" approach walks alongside low-income people, starting with the biblical truth that they are image bearers. Yes, they are broken, just as we all are. But this brokenness does not negate the fact that they retain the image of God and have gifts, resources, and abilities that they are called and empowered to steward. An asset-based approach does not ignore the needs of materially poor individuals and communities but seeks to identify, celebrate, and mobilize their own gifts, abilities, and resources as much as possible to address those needs and to serve others.

Note that using an asset-based approach does not mean a ministry should never give resources or other forms of material help to materially poor people, but rather that it should only do so in a way that builds upon, not undermines, their use of their own gifts, abilities, and resources. Unfortunately, because we Westerners are materialistic people, we tend to reduce poverty to a lack of material things and to think that material things can solve all problems. Hence, we often provide resources too soon and in too large quantities; and in the process, we undermine the ability of materially poor people to use their own gifts, abilities, and resources.

An asset-based approach can help prevent the unhealthy god-complex-marred-identity-handouts dynamic captured in the following equation:

Material Definition of Poverty	+	Feelings of Superiority of Materially Non-Poor	+	Feelings of Inferiority of Materially Poor	=	Harm to both Materially Poor and Non-Poor

Focusing on the assets that God has given low-income people frames our interactions with them, reminding us that they too are called to the community of priest-kings who are spreading the knowledge and worship of God. In the process, it fosters an attitude of respect in our hearts for low-income people, countering our sense of superiority and our tendency to feel that we need to fix them. And it affirms in the materially poor that they have gifts they are called to steward, thereby combating their feelings of inferiority and calling them to take responsibility for declaring His praises.

An asset-based approach opens our eyes to possibilities that neither the materially poor nor non-poor might have seen otherwise. For example, when the microfinance movement began, it was dominated by a credit-led approach: Westerners set up large microfinance institutions staffed by professionals that lent Western money to poor people and collected it back with interest. Although this approach has some strengths, it also has numerous weaknesses: it cannot reach the poorest people; is often inflexible; struggles to get to rural areas; is heavily dependent on outside managerial, technical, and financial resources; and fails to provide some additional financial services that poor people need—like savings accounts.

Indeed, had the industry pursued a more asset-based approach, it could have overcome these problems. For example, to the surprise of many of the initial leaders of this movement, poor people can and do save. In fact, many of them would prefer to save rather than borrow, for saving is less risky. In addition, poor people have the ability to manage savings and credit associations on their own. In fact, these associations are indigenous to most Majority World countries. So while outsiders can provide a valuable service through training that strengthens the functioning of these groups, such training is building on the knowledge that people already have. The result is that even poor churches in Kenya are able to use *Restore: Savings*—the Chalmers Center's church-based savings and credit association curriculum—to equip fifty HIV/AIDS sufferers, some of the poorest and most despised people on earth, to use their own financial and social capital, their indigenous knowledge, and the power of Jesus Christ and His indwelling Spirit to holistically minister to a thousand of the poorest people on the planet (see chapter 1). Amazingly, these groups overcome the weaknesses of the credit-led financial institutions mentioned earlier, for they can reach the poorest people; are highly flexible; can work in rural areas; are not dependent on outside managerial, technical, and financial resources; and provide both loans and savings services.

Sometimes even apparent weaknesses can be turned into assets. Like several members of my own family, Bob struggles with obsessive compulsive disorder. Yes, this is a problem, but it also means that Bob actually enjoys cleaning and is pretty good at it. So, we helped Bob to get going on a house cleaning business, calling it *O.ver C.oming D.irt: Putting My Obsessions to Work for You!* God can even turn our broken parts into assets that can be used for His glory.

Before you start any ministry with a materially poor individual or community, find out what assets they have and seek to mobilize those assets.[6]

> **Questions for Reflection:**
> 1. What is your ministry doing to identify, mobilize, and connect the assets and abilities of low-income people or communities? What specific things could you do in this regard?
>
> _____
>
> _____
>
> _____
>
> _____

2. Do you see your materially non-poor stakeholders becoming more or less prideful over time?

_____

_____

_____

_____

3. Do you see your materially poor stakeholders growing in their dignity as image bearers?

_____

_____

_____

_____

4. Do you see your materially poor stakeholders increasingly using their own gifts and abilities?

_____

_____

_____

_____

Practices
Replacing destructive
formative practices

Ministry Design Principle 12: Use participatory rather than blueprint approaches.
Poverty alleviation is about change, and in order for a low-income individual or community to pursue the hard road of making changes in their lives, it is profoundly important that they "own" the course of action from the very beginning. This means that both Bob and those of us who are walking with him must see him as the person who is primarily responsible for making these changes happen. And like most human beings, materially poor people generally "own" plans that they have helped to initiate and to shape more than plans that have been imposed upon them.

Hence, poverty alleviation efforts should avoid "blueprint" approaches that impose a predetermined plan on low-income people, imposing our ideas about what to do and how it should be done. A blueprint approach fails to create the necessary ownership of the change process that is essential if materially poor people are going to initiate and sustain the necessary changes in their lives. In addition, a blueprint approach tends to exacerbate the harmful dynamic in which the materially non-poor "play god," speaking and acting in ways that confirm the sense of inferiority and shame that many low-income people already feel.

Conversely, a participatory approach asks Bob what he believes he should do to improve his life, how he thinks he should do it, and what actions he will take to pursue positive change. This does not mean that we should never speak into Bob's life, but simply that we should try to act in a way that is consistent with biblical truth: as an image bearer, Bob has insights and abilities, and he is called by God to be the primary person who stewards those insights and abilities, using them to initiate and sustain changes that move toward becoming whole.

Of course, change is possible only if a person is willing to change, and people vary widely in their receptivity to change. If Bob does not believe that change is possible, if he is unwilling to go through the pain of change, or if he does not believe that he is the person who is primarily responsible for making the necessary changes in his life, it will be very difficult to make progress with him. Remember, while we have a crucial role to play in the life of a materially poor individual or community, we cannot change them. Rather, our role is to encourage them as they initiate and drive their own change process through the power of the Holy Spirit.

One of the most challenging elements of poverty alleviation is identifying those people who are truly ready to change. While there is no magic formula for this, one approach that often helps is to ensure that all the stakeholders—including the materially poor people—have "skin in the game" as soon as possible, for people are usually unwilling to contribute to things that they do not really embrace. For example, when the Chalmers Center trains poor churches in the Majority World to start microfinance ministries, we charge them something to be trained. These churches are extremely poor, so the amount they pay covers only a small fraction of the overall training costs, but that doesn't matter. It would be okay if they contributed a chicken's foot as long as they were giving up something that is valuable to them.

Similarly, when a person walks into your church and asks for help with paying their electric bill, having them complete an "action plan" can serve both to increase their sense of ownership in their own pathway forward and to diagnose how serious they are about making positive changes. An action plan asks the person to commit to taking specific steps to achieve their own goals, and your ministry agrees to provide appropriate support, encouragement, and accountability to complement the person's efforts. If a person isn't willing to spend time completing such a plan and just wants quick cash, it suggests they are not serious about making long-term changes. For more on this, see *Helping Without Hurting in Church Benevolence: A Practical Guide to Walking with Low-Income People* by Steve Corbett and Brian Fikkert with Katie Casselberry.

While participation increases ownership and hence makes the poverty alleviation initiative more likely to succeed, it is a mistake to view participation solely as a means of achieving that end. Why? It all goes back to God's story of change. Remember, the goal is to restore people to experiencing humanness in the way that God intended. The crucial thing is to help people understand they are priest-kings who are called to love their neighbors as themselves, to be stewards over God's creation, and to bring glory to God in all things. This requires that people steward their individual lives and communities, constantly seeking better ways to use their gifts and resources to solve problems and to create bounty in service to God and others. This means people are empowered to make decisions about the best way to steward their resources, to act upon their decisions, to evaluate the results of their decisions, and then to start the decision-making process all over again. In this light, participation is not just a means to an end but the most important end!

Questions for Reflection:

1. How much input are you receiving from materially poor people about your ministry?

_____

_____

_____

_____

2. Do all the stakeholders have "skin in the game?" If not, what could you do to change this?

_____

_____

_____

_____

3. How could you increase the participation of materially poor people in the selection, design, execution, and evaluation of your ministry?

_____

_____

_____

_____

Practices
Replacing destructive
formative practices

Ministry Design Principle 13: All interventions should be pro work.

This principle is really just a corollary to several others, but we are stating it explicitly because it is too often overlooked by the Christian community.

Enabling materially poor people to engage in work that pays a living wage is the most sustainable way for them to no longer be materially poor. Period.

Take Bob, for example. If he could work and earn enough money, he wouldn't have to waste enormous amounts of time and energy asking for help from one church and social service agency after another, most of which are not really set up to help him. Moreover, he could pay the rent on an apartment so he wouldn't be homeless any more. Finally, he could afford to get the physical and mental health care he needs. God ordained work as the primary way for people to provide for themselves and to have something to share with others (see Gen. 1:28–29; Eph. 4:28). Work is absolutely essential to ending material poverty.

And as we have seen, work is not just a means to an end: being able to eat. On the contrary, one of the central features of being a priest-king—one of the central features of being human—is to spread the reign and worship of God through work. We have pictured this idea by the *relationship with creation* spoke in the wheel. When people cannot engage in sustaining work, this spoke is removed, and the whole wheel becomes distorted. The absence of work negatively impacts every aspect of the human being. Work is absolutely essential to becoming whole.

Unfortunately, research has found that while American churches typically provide food, temporary housing, and clothing to help materially poor people, only 2 percent devote resources to helping them work.[7] Churches treat the symptoms—the inability to buy food, housing, and clothing—rather than getting to the underlying reasons that the poor people are unable to buy these necessities in the first place.

Certainly, helping people engage in sustaining work is more difficult than ladling out soup to them, but, as the examples in this book illustrate, it is more than possible: it is already happening! Churches and parachurch ministries all over the world and across the US are using microfinance, jobs preparedness, financial education, and small business training to restore people to work that is dignifying, sustainable, and God-glorifying.

Of course, other types of ministries are still needed. Because people are whole people, they need health care, trauma counseling, housing, Bible studies, emergency assistance, clean water, malaria nets, and so on. A host of issues need to be addressed. But all these ministries should be designed in a way that is consistent with restoring people to sustaining work.

For example, when Bob explains to churches that he is homeless, a little bit of creativity on the part of those churches would go a long way. Instead of writing checks for Bob to pay the costs of a motel, the church could agree to pay Bob to work part-time at the church or at a nonprofit ministry. Rather than writing the paychecks to Bob, the church could write the checks directly to the motel or to a landlord to ensure that the money goes to pay for housing. This is a pro-work way of solving Bob's housing problem that would help him recover a sense of dignity, put him into contact with supportive people, get him back into the habit of working, and move him toward becoming whole.

Questions for Reflection:

1. Is your ministry helping people engage in sustaining work?

_____

_____

_____

_____

2. Can you think of any creative ways that your ministry could become more pro-work?

_____

_____

_____

_____

Practices

Replacing destructive
formative practices

Ministry Design Principle 14: Encourage all stakeholders to give sacrificially.

The love that exists from all eternity between the Father, Son, and Spirit overflows in self-sacrificial generosity. Sent out of the love of the Father, the Son freely comes in the power and fellowship of the Spirit; therefore, in the cross we see the clearest manifestation of God's self-giving love and grace. This is why the cross becomes the greatest symbol for shaping our imagination of what it means to follow God and imitate Christ (see Mark 8:34; John 15:12–13; Eph. 5:1–2; 1 Peter 2:21; 1 John 3:16).[8]

So, as we grow more and more into our skin as image bearers of this loving God—as we become increasingly whole—we will give sacrificially as well. The fact that sacrificial giving is central to human flourishing turns standard approaches to poverty alleviation upside down. In both Western Naturalism and Evangelical Gnosticism, human flourishing in this life comes from greater consumption. Indeed, the primary metric that economists use to evaluate the effectiveness of a poverty alleviation initiative is the extent to which the program increases poor households' consumption expenditures. Of course, there is considerable merit in using this metric, because people who are extremely poor typically do need more food, clothing, shelter, and so on. But human flourishing entails more than just consuming. If we want to promote true human flourishing, then our poverty alleviation ministries should encourage poor people to give sacrificially to others. In fact, one could argue that one of the primary measures of success in our poverty alleviation ministries should be the extent to which sacrificial giving is increasing for all the stakeholders: the poor people, the staff, the volunteers, and the donors.

There is no one-size-fits-all formula for what this giving should look like. But the ministry should encourage all the stakeholders to give time, treasure, or talents in service to others in some fashion. And don't shy away from asking poor people to give sacrificially. The poorest people on the planet can and do give generously to others on a regular basis, and as they do so, they become more whole.[9]

Questions for Reflection:

1. Are there any ways in which your ministry disciples its stakeholders (financial supporters, staff, and materially poor people) to understand and practice the joy of sacrificial giving?

_____

_____

_____

_____

2. What specific actions will you take to improve your ministry's discipleship of its stakeholders in this regard?

_____

_____

_____

_____

Practices
Replacing destructive formative practices

Ministry Design Principle 15: Foster whole-person discipleship using adult education training techniques.

Most poverty alleviation ministries include some type of training for the materially poor participants. Unfortunately, in some ways, Westerners are particularly ill-suited for this task.

As we explored in *Becoming Whole* chapter 4, when Western civilization recognizes something akin to a soul, it often reduces the multifaceted soul to the mind. Additionally, Western educators tend to value the mind over the body, so students are perceived simply as "brains on sticks." Consequently, Western teaching tends to use a lecture-based style in which the teacher tries to pour content into the students' brains.

A lecture-based style can be quite harmful in the space of poverty alleviation. When a materially non-poor teacher stands at the front of a room of materially poor participants and does all the talking, it can exacerbate the god-complex-marred-identity dynamic. This style of teaching reinforces the idea that the materially non-poor are superior, that they are not broken, and that they have all the answers. And it reinforces the idea that the materially poor are inferior and have nothing to contribute. Worse yet, in the context of former colonies, this style is eerily reminiscent of the ones used in the educational systems established by the Western colonizers.

In addition, given that people are mind-affections-will-body-relational creatures, we would expect pedagogical approaches that engage the whole person would be more effective than a lecture-based style. And indeed this is the case. Using brain imaging techniques, researchers are finding that transformative learning occurs when human beings engage in a repeated *action-reflection cycle* that impacts not just what people think (mind), but also what they feel (affections) and do (will).[10] Discipleship isn't about content dump; it's about engaging the whole person in an ongoing cycle of narrating truth, engaging in formative practices, and reflecting on experiences. Along these lines, we discover the Christian life is not just about learning truths, but about living them. Christianity isn't just about ideas, it's about relationships with God and others. As we said before, true Christianity doesn't choose between belief and action, between content and engagement; Christians participate in an active belief—a lived faith.

Adult education is an approach that seeks to engage the whole person in this type of ongoing action-reflection cycle.[11] In particular, Jane Vella and the organization she founded, Global Learning Partners, have developed "dialogue education," a set of principles that have informed the development of the training and curricula featured in this *Field Guide*.[12]

Facilitation is one of the key tools of dialogue education. As summarized in Table 5.3, facilitation is different from teaching in that it levels the playing field, respecting the knowledge, experiences, and contributions of all the participants. In other words, it is far more asset-based and participatory than traditional teaching, thereby helping to overcome the god-complex-marred-identity dynamic. This approach can be particularly powerful if the "students" include both materially poor and non-poor people, as is often the case with *Faith & Finances*. Through highly engaging activities and reflective questions digested in the context of a supportive community, walls start to break down and participants slowly start to embrace the good news of God's story of change: all of us are broken and all of us are in the process of being restored to something that looks fundamentally different from the American Dream.

TABLE 5.3
Facilitation versus Teaching

FACILITATION	TEACHING
1. Values personal experience	1. Values facts and knowledge
2. Everyone contributes to the learning	2. Teacher gives students information
3. Participants and facilitator share power in the learning environment	3. Teacher holds all the power in a classroom style setting
4. Aims to create a safe environment for sharing experiences	4. Creates fear of authority or teacher
5. Based on respect for each other and shared responsibility between participants	5. Values obedience and "good behavior"
6. Encourages risk-taking and diversity of experiences	6. Focuses on correct answers and success
7. Values cooperation among participants	7. Fosters competition between students
8. Values emotions as well as logical thinking	8. Values logical thinking and ignores emotion
9. Encourages creative thinking	9. Values memory-based learning
10. Focuses on building skills that affect one's personal life	10. Usually focuses on giving theoretical knowledge

Derived from D. Naker and L. Michau, *Rethinking Domestic Violence: A Training Process for Community Activists* (Kampala, Uganda: Raising Voices, 2004), 13.

Furthermore, dialogue education views real learning as impacting participants' knowledge (mind), attitudes (affections), practices (will), and even bodies in a learning community that is highly relational and supportive. This is education for the whole person in an ongoing action-reflection cycle across time, making it consistent with biblical anthropology and discipleship. For example, when a *Faith & Finances* group meets, the lesson is constructed around the "4As" of dialogue education:

1. *Anchor:* connect the topic to a relevant experience in the lives of the participants.
2. *Add:* supply new information (technical content, for example) and invite participants to think about the implications of this information for their relevant experience.
3. *Apply:* provide an opportunity for participants to think about what they could do with the new information to improve their life experience.
4. *Away:* ask participants to commit to taking specific actions to change their life experience.[13]

And at the next meeting, the cycle repeats itself, helping people to continue on their journey to becoming whole.

Questions for Reflection:
1. If your ministry does any training, does it use a lecture teaching style or more of a facilitation style?

_____

_____

_____

2. Do program participants find your ministry's training to be solicitous of their knowledge and experiences, or do your trainers act like they are the ones with all the insights?

_____

_____

_____

3. What specific action will you take to improve your staff's facilitation skills?

_____

_____

_____

BOB THE PRIEST-KING

The first weekend that Bob was staying with us, my wife had to go out of town. Bob volunteered to clean our house, so I decided to spend Saturday working on this book. As I typed away in my study, Bob vacuumed, dusted, and mopped, muttering under his breath the entire time. It seemed a little strange to me, and I wondered whether he had an imaginary friend.

When we sat down to eat supper together, I asked Bob who he had been talking to all day. He said, "I was talking to God the whole time. I thanked Him for getting me up this morning and for giving me a place to stay. And I kept asking Him to help me do a good job cleaning your house. Basically, I just tried to be with Him all day. That's how I try to do things." Meanwhile, I had been feeling sorry for myself all day about the fact that I was having to work.

The next morning when I came downstairs, I found a handwritten note from Bob on the kitchen table: "Brian, wouldn't it be nice if you had a bouquet of flowers waiting for Jill when she gets home? I think you should put them right here." And at the bottom of the note, he had drawn an arrow pointing to the exact spot where I should place the flowers. (P.S., I bought her flowers!)

Bob has a lot of ups and downs, and sometimes it's tough to see whether his life is trending in the right direction. But that weekend, Bob modeled for me what it means to be a priest-king: dwelling in God's presence, engaging in God-glorifying work, and loving others. Like all God's children, Bob is in process, a process that God promises to complete, a process in which Bob is undoubtedly becoming whole (see Phil. 1:6; 1 Thess. 5:23–24).

CHAPTER SIX

ADDRESSING BROKEN SYSTEMS AND BROKEN PEOPLE

Most white evangelicals, directed by their cultural tools, fail to recognize the institutionalization of racialization—in economic, political, educational, social, and religion systems. They therefore often think and act as if these problems do not exist.[1]

—MICHAEL EMERSON AND CHRISTIAN SMITH, COAUTHORS OF *DIVIDED BY FAITH*, 2001

Because of the savings group and through the teaching we are receiving, I have accepted Jesus as my Lord and Savior. And He has changed my life.[2]

—MEMBER OF CHURCH-CENTERED SAVINGS AND CREDIT ASSOCIATION IN TOGO, 2012

There are both internal and external causes of relational and material poverty. Systems are broken, and individuals are broken. Moreover, these factors are often so intertwined that it is difficult to sort them out.[3] Yes, Absco, Joy, Maurice, Cindy, and Bob are responsible for their own behaviors, but it is easy to see that the cards were stacked against them.

Actually, there is a sense in which the cards are stacked against all of us. *While those of us who are not materially poor should never compare our struggles with those who are,* the truth is that broken systems have damaged all of us, albeit in different ways. None of us chose to be born into the communities that have enculturated us to *automatically* and *unconsciously* think, feel, and act in the ways that we do. Just

125

as materially poor people are deeply shaped by the systems of their communities, so are the materially non-poor. Indeed, being highly individualistic, self-centered materialists comes quite naturally for many of us who were raised in Western civilization. It's not so much that we consciously chose to be like this; somehow the materialistic values embedded in the systems of our mainstream culture—the ubiquitous media, the sprawling mega-malls, and the stampeding financial markets—just sort of seeped into our DNA by osmosis. Hence, while we are always morally responsible, in many ways we didn't consciously choose our way of being. It all just seems normal to us. We usually don't even realize that there are any alternatives.

In other words, we all need liberation from systemic and personal brokenness. The only difference is that the materially poor often realize they need it, while the materially non-poor generally do not.

THE KINGDOM COMMUNITY: ADDRESSING BROKEN SYSTEMS

The first step in fixing broken systems is realizing they are broken. And this is where many evangelical Christians get tripped up. In their pathbreaking book, *Divided by Faith*, sociologists Michael Emerson and Christian Smith report on their extensive research about American attitudes toward race and poverty. Sadly, white evangelical Christians are the group in America least likely to believe that broken systems contribute to racial injustice and poverty. Despite its professed commitment to the Bible, this group has apparently not read the major or minor prophets, who rail against God's people for ignoring oppressive systems. The effects of the fall are cosmic in scope, but somehow so many white evangelicals think the fall has impacted only individuals' hearts.

As Emerson and Smith document, white evangelicals have often justified the status quo, even when that status quo included a system that was straight from the bowels of hell: the enslavement of African Americans. Although most evangelicals today would agree that slavery was wrong, Emerson and Smith show that white evangelicals continue to be blind to the ongoing role of broken systems as a cause of poverty and racial injustice. The reasons for this blindness are complex, but Emerson and Smith argue that the fundamental problem is that most white evangelicals are "accountable freewill individualists." As such, they believe that individuals are "independent of structures and institutions, have free will, and are individually accountable for their own actions."[4] In addition, the strong evangelical commitment to a personal relationship with Jesus Christ and to individual piety has narrowed the scope of evangelicals' concerns so that social structures are simply off the radar screen.[5]

While it is certainly true that the Bible always holds individuals accountable for their own thoughts and actions, it is inconsistent with biblical revelation to view people as "independent of structures and institutions." Just as a wheel is shaped by the road on which it travels, we mind-affections-will-body-relational creatures are necessarily impacted by our environments, including the formal and informal systems of our cultural surroundings. Indeed, the Bible warns us about the corrupting power of the people and systems around us:

> Bad company corrupts good character. (1 Cor. 15:33)

> Do not conform to the pattern of this world, but be transformed by the renewing of your mind. Then you will be able to test and approve what God's will is— his good, pleasing and perfect will. (Rom. 12:2)

Environment matters, both for the materially poor and non-poor. In addition, while personal piety is extremely important, God detests such piety when it doesn't lead to a concern for social justice:

> I hate, I despise your religious festivals; your assemblies are a stench to me. Even though you bring me burnt offerings and grain offerings, I will not accept them. Though you bring choice fellowship offerings, I will have no regard for them. Away with the noise

of your songs! I will not listen to the music of your harps. But let justice roll on like a river, righteousness like a never-failing stream! (Amos 5:21–24)

Christ died to liberate the entire cosmos. Who are we to limit His concerns to personal piety?

Systems

Addressing broken systems

Ministry Design Principle 16: Address broken systems by navigating existing ones, creating alternatives, and/or reforming them altogether.

For many of us, the systems work relatively well, at least in terms of enabling us to make a living. This fact, combined with the theological blindness described earlier, means that many of us are often unaware of how the systems are broken. Hence, the first step is to try to identify the systems that are creating obstacles for the materially poor people we are trying to help.

One way to do this is by walking in relationship with poor people across time, seeing how the world looks through their eyes, watching their behaviors, and accompanying them as they try to make the systems work for themselves. For example, you might tag along as a low-income friend goes grocery shopping. Depending on the situation, you may encounter a "food desert," an absence of grocery stores, that requires the person to travel several miles just to buy vegetables. And due to a lack of public transportation, you may find yourself walking these miles with your friend—in the rain. While you are walking, you might ask your friend why they don't move to a place closer to the grocery store, and suddenly the issues of affordable housing, racial discrimination, mortgage lending practices, educational disparities, and employment discrimination will be on the table. We need to spend some time to see the world through the eyes of our materially poor friends and neighbors.[6]

Once you've identified a broken system that your ministry will seek to address, there are several options for how to proceed.

First, you might be able to find ways to help materially poor people better navigate the existing systems. This is the approach of *Faith*

& Finances. By helping participants understand the dangers of various types of predatory lenders, how to calculate interest rates, and the benefits of bank accounts, *Faith & Finances* helps people walk through the minefield of systems without stepping on the mines, largely through bringing low-income participants into relationship with middle-income allies who are familiar with the ins and outs of the banking system.

Second, sometimes a ministry can create alternative systems on a micro level. This is the essence of the savings and credit associations described earlier. Financial systems are profoundly inadequate for poor people in the Majority World. Banks are often unavailable, especially in rural areas. And even when there are banks, poor people typically cannot meet the minimum balance requirements for savings accounts, and they lack acceptable collateral to be able to borrow. As a result, poor people are often at the mercy of loan sharks, who lend them money at exorbitant interest rates.

Savings and credit associations are like mini-banks that poor people own and operate themselves. While a single association will not change the entire banking system, it does create an alternative system for the group members whom the ministry is trying to help. And sometimes things can grow over time. For example, it is extremely common for savings and credit associations to self-replicate. A church in a neighboring village might ask the members of an existing savings and credit association to train their church to start a similar ministry. And then it can spread to another village after that. "Do not despise these small beginnings" (Zech. 4:10 NLT).[7]

Third, some ministries may be called to address broken systems by trying to reform them altogether. One such approach is called "community organizing," a process that develops the local leadership, relationships, and momentum to bring wide-scale change to the systems affecting a community. More information about this approach can be found in *When Helping Hurts*.[8] In addition, some ministries may be called to advocate for systemic change at a more macro level, seeking to reform the institutions for the entire society.

A recent resource that seeks to help Christians working at this level is *Advocating for Justice: An Evangelical Vision for Transforming Systems and Structures,* edited by Stephen Offutt.

Questions for Reflection:

1. Can you think of any ways in which systems have encultur-ated you to *automatically* and even *unconsciously* think, feel, or act in certain ways? Which of these ways are consistent with God's story of change, and which are more reflective of the "pattern of the world"?

_____

_____

_____

2. Has your poverty alleviation ministry explored ways that bro-ken systems may be contributing to the material poverty of the people whom it is seeking to help? What does the minis-try commit to do to learn more about this matter?

_____

_____

_____

3. Has your ministry expressed empathy to poor people about any ways that broken systems have contributed to their situation?

_____

_____

_____

4. What specifically is your poverty alleviation ministry doing to address broken systems? Are there any additional actions it could take?

_____

_____

_____

5. Should your ministry pursue navigating, creating alternatives, or reforming?

_____

_____

_____

THE KINGDOM COMMUNITY: ADDRESSING BROKEN PEOPLE

Because our individual personhoods can be impacted by all five causes of poverty, fixing any part of the community can help address individual brokenness. For example, if systemic racial discrimination ends, then more materially poor people will be able to get jobs. The resulting restoration of their relationship to creation amounts to putting one of the spokes in the wheel back into place, thereby causing them to be less broken. Every aspect of our individual personhoods—our minds, affections, wills, bodies, and relationships—are deeply shaped by the story of change, practices, systems, and demonic forces operating within our culture.

Consider the following question that I recently included on a college test:

_____(True/False) The story of change in the culture in which we live impacts our intestines.

The answer to this question is "True." As depicted in Figure 1.3, our individual personhoods, including our bodies, are impacted by the cultures in which we live. As the people in a culture pursue that culture's goals and ways of achieving those goals, they engage in practices and create systems that impact every aspect of the highly integrated mind-affections-will-body-relational creature, right down to people's intestines. For example, researchers have found that growing up in an environment with oppressive systems often has devastating physical and emotional consequences that can last a lifetime.[9] If we want to bring healing to broken people, often much outside of them needs to be fixed.

That said, some things can and *must* be done to directly address broken individuals, even as we seek to address the other portions of the community that impact them. And it is those very direct measures that will be discussed in this section.

People

Addressing broken people

Ministry Design Principle 17: Help people access physical and mental health care.

One of the results of the fall is that our minds, affections, wills, and bodies are not completely healthy, which can dramatically contribute to material poverty. Sick or physically weak people understandably find it difficult to work, and a host of mental health issues can impair people's functionality, including their ability to earn a living.

And sometimes it all just snowballs: lower incomes and rising health expenditures increase the household's physical and emotional stress, which can lead to additional health problems. In response, extremely poor people may cut back on eating to make ends meet, which further weakens them both physically and mentally. Over time, families can be caught in what economists call a poverty trap, an inescapable downward spiral: illness leads to poverty, which leads to more illness, which leads to more poverty.

Seeking to understand the causes of poverty, Anirudh Krishna, Professor of Public Policy and Political Science at Duke University, spearheaded interviews with 35,000 households in India, Kenya, Uganda, Peru, and the United States. Krishna summarizes his findings in his book *One Illness Away: Why People Become Poor and How They Escape Poverty.* Included in the book is the story of Heera Gujar, a farmer in Rajasthan, India, who describes his experiences as follows:

> We were among the more prosperous households
> of our village. We owned land. We also owned many
> heads of cattle. But things changed for the worse,
> and today we are among the poorest people in our
> village, the recipients of community handouts on
> religious holidays.

The bad days began when my father fell ill about 18 years ago. They say he was stricken by TB [tuberculosis]. We took him several times to the district hospital, about 35 kilometers away. Each time we spent a considerable amount of money. We must have spent close to 25,000 rupees on his treatment, but to no avail. When my father died, we performed the customary death feast, spending another 10,000 rupees. We sold our cattle, and we also had to take out some loans. We worked harder in order to repay these debts. Then, about ten years ago, my wife fell seriously ill, and she has still not recovered. We borrowed more money to pay for her medical treatments. More than 20,000 rupees were spent for this purpose. It became hard to keep up with our debts. Somehow we could make due for another two or three years. Then the rains failed for three years in a row, and that was the end of the road for us. We sold our land.

Now, my sons and I work as casual labor, earning whatever we can from one day to the next. On some days, we find work. On other days, there is nothing.[10]

As Krishna explains, Heera's story is all too common:

Several other factors are also associated with falling into poverty, but in terms of frequency and magnitude, the effects of ill-health and health care expenses predominate in every region examined. Ill-health—when high treatment costs go together with loss of earning power—imposes a double burden on households and it has the biggest influence on becoming poor (and remaining in poverty).[11]

Often, relatively low-cost preventative care can prevent physical and mental crises, so there is a desperate need to expand community health education. Nevertheless, when God presents us with fifty HIV/AIDS sufferers or with a homeless person struggling with mental health issues, helping them access health care for their bodies and minds is essential to helping them become whole.

Questions for Reflection:

1. What types of physical or mental health care are needed by the people with whom your ministry is walking? How could your ministry help them to obtain such care?

_____

_____

_____

_____

2. What could your ministry do to help people prepare for health emergencies?

_____

_____

_____

_____

People
Addressing broken people

Ministry Design Principle 18: Verbally invite unbelievers to saving faith in Jesus Christ.

Many of the benefits of Christ's kingdom are enjoyed by both believers and unbelievers: God sends sunlight and rain to all people (Matt. 5:45). Moreover, the community of restored priest-kings should seek to extend the benefits of His kingdom to all out of a posture of love, humility, and grace. This means that when the public school system is broken, Christians should work to fix it out of love for all children, even if our kids are in Christian schools. And when gentrification drives materially poor people out of the neighborhood, we should work for greater justice in housing for all people, whether they are believers or unbelievers. King Jesus reigns, and His love should permeate His entire kingdom.

There should be no community more welcoming to sinners of all types, including to Pharisees like ourselves, than God's family. Indeed, our outpouring of love and grace to all should be so dramatic that the world comes running, not just to us, but to our King (Matt. 5:16).

Indeed, they need to come to our King, in faith and repentance. For as we have seen, the foundation for human flourishing—both in this life and the next—is being brought back into communion with God, and only the work of Jesus Christ and the Holy Spirit can get us there. As Jesus says, "I am the way and the truth and the life. No one comes to the Father except through me" (John 14:6). There are no substitutes, and there are no alternatives. Jesus is the only way to enter the dwelling place of God, the only person in whom all five causes of both relational and material poverty are defeated. And we are dependent on the Spirit to move, to open eyes and ears, to hear our prayers, and to act. If you truly want to help materially poor people escape poverty, you must help them get home. This means we must pray in dependence on the Spirit and seek to introduce them to the risen King.

Do not make the mistake of thinking that being brought back into communion with God impacts only our souls. As we have seen, being restored to a right relationship with God is like having the top spoke in our wheel restored; it impacts every aspect of our beings: our bodies, souls, and relationships (see Figure 6.1). Without such restoration, humans simply cannot fully flourish. Being restored to the dwelling place of God is foundational for successful poverty alleviation—for truly becoming whole.

FIGURE 6.1

The Restoration of the Human Being

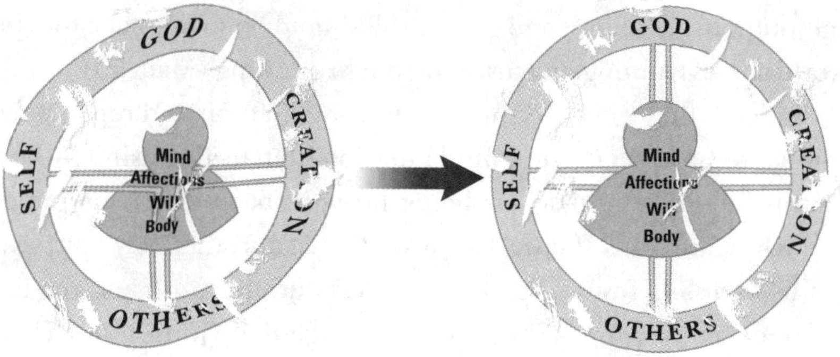

Adapted from Brian Fikkert and Russell Mask, *From Dependence to Dignity: How to Alleviate Poverty through Church-Centered Microfinance* (Grand Rapids: Zondervan, 2015), 91.

And this requires us to verbally communicate the gospel to unbelievers, for faith comes through hearing the word about Christ:

> "Everyone who calls on the name of the Lord will be saved."
>
> How, then, can they call on the one they have not believed in? And how can they believe in the one of whom they have not heard? And how can they hear without someone preaching to them? And how can anyone preach unless they are sent? As it is written: "How beautiful are the feet of those who bring good news!"
>
> But not all the Israelites accepted the good news. For Isaiah says, "Lord, who has believed our message?" *Consequently, faith comes from hearing the message, and the message is heard through the word about Christ.* (Rom. 10:13–17, emphasis added)

These biblical truths present a challenge to those who are passionate about social justice but disinterested in evangelism. From a biblical perspective, full human flourishing is impossible without being united to Jesus Christ. He is the only One who can address the deepest longings of our soul—to be returned to the dwelling place of God. Moreover, it is only those who are *in Christ* who get to fully experience the benefits of His kingdom, both now and for all eternity. Hence, saving faith is absolutely essential for human flourishing, and God has ordained the verbal articulation of the gospel as the normal means that He uses to draw people into saving faith. Using words to communicate the gospel is absolutely essential for true poverty alleviation—for helping people to become whole.

Of course, we should not presume that all materially poor people are unbelievers. Indeed, the typical Christian in the twenty-first century is an extremely poor person living in the Majority World. Remember, there are multiple causes for material poverty, not just the behaviors that sometimes result from individual brokenness. To believe that materially poor people are necessarily unbelievers is to embrace the erroneous teachings of the health-and-wealth gospel.[12]

We must also state that the most effective way to verbally share the gospel depends on the context (see 1 Cor. 9:19–23). What works in the Bible Belt would usually not work well in a Muslim setting. And showing cultural sensitivity honors the whole person, communicating that their entire being and culture are of value.

Finally, the gospel must be communicated in its fullness. People need to understand that they are sinners who need to be declared righteous before a holy God. And they also need to know that salvation brings them into a family, makes them new creatures in Christ, restores them as priest-kings, and launches them on the path to becoming whole. This is more than a three-minute conversation: the gospel is the good news of the kingdom, and the kingdom is big.

Questions for Reflection:
1. What is your own attitude to verbally sharing the gospel?

_____

_____

_____

_____

_____

2. What are the intentional ways that your ministry verbally shares the gospel with unbelievers? Are these ways culturally appropriate? How could you strengthen your ministry in this area?

_____

_____

_____

_____

_____

_____

3. Reflect on the message that your ministry is communicating with respect to the gospel. Are there any ways in which your ministry is communicating only that people need to be declared righteous before a holy God? Alternatively, are there any ways in which your ministry is communicating only some of the benefits of the gospel without emphasizing the need to be forgiven of one's sins? How can your ministry better communicate the gospel in its fullness?

_____

_____

_____

_____

People

Addressing
broken people

Ministry Design Principle 19: Invite people into the church's administration of the ordinary means of grace.

In many ways, this is a corollary to *Ministry Design Principle 1: Christian poverty alleviation ministries must be rrooted in and lead back to the local church.*

Like all of us, materially poor believers and unbelievers need to encounter the very person of Jesus Christ. And when the church assembles under its God-ordained leadership for the administration of the ordinary means of grace—the preaching of the Word, the sacraments, and prayer—Christ has promised to be personally present by His Spirit. And this is truly good news, for we need Jesus, not just an idea about Him, but *Him*! All of us—including materially poor people—need to experience the power of His presence, holiness, and love. We need his forgiveness and grace. There is nothing like resting in God's benediction. He is the answer to poverty. He alone can make us whole. And He really is present with us when the local church faithfully administers the ordinary means of grace.

The Way to Achieve the Goal of the Biblical Story of Change

Through the gift of the Son and Spirit, the triune God accomplishes our reconciliation to God, self, others, and the rest of creation.

While unbelievers can encounter the very presence of Christ in the preaching of the Word, they should not partake of the Lord's Supper (1 Cor. 11:29). This does not mean they should be absent when it is served, however, for it is a powerful declaration of the gospel to say to unbelievers, "This is for God's family. You aren't a member yet, but why don't you come home?"

For example, Redeemer Presbyterian Church in New York City, founded by Pastor Tim Keller, includes short prayers in the bulletin that unbelievers can read during the Lord's Supper:

> "We invite everybody to do business with God," Keller says to the congregation. "We are not excluding anybody. You who are not yet believers should not partake, but we invite you to do business with God."
>
> One hundred or more first-time visitors attend Redeemer Presbyterian every Sunday. At first Tim Keller thought that would present major obstacles to serving the Lord's Supper.
>
> "I discovered an amazing thing, though," says Keller. "When the Lord's Supper comes around, the

unbeliever is forced to ask, 'Where am I?' Communion is a specific and extremely visible way to see the difference between walking with Christ and living for yourself. The Lord's Supper confronts people with the questions: Are you right with God today? On which side of the line are you?"

One woman came up to Keller after a service and said, "I've been coming here for three months. I thought I was a Christian when I started coming, even though I hadn't gone to church since I was a little girl. I haven't come here every week, so somehow I missed other Communion services. When I got here today, I read the things about Communion in the bulletin and realized that I wasn't sure I was a Christian."

She decided she wanted to make sure. She gave her life to Christ as the bread and cup were being shared. She participated in Communion and told Keller that she felt her whole life changed.

"I don't think there's any more effective way to help a person do a spiritual inventory," says Keller. "Many seekers in the United States will realize they are non-Christians only during the Lord's Supper. At our church we may begin doing the Lord's Supper more often because we're realizing what a powerful evangelistic tool it is."[13]

Like all of us, materially poor people need the healing power of Jesus. And He is present—mysteriously yet really—when the church administers the ordinary means of grace. This is the innermost sanctuary of the temple, the very dwelling place of God. We are home there. And home is where we become whole.

Questions for Reflection:

1. Is your ministry intentionally connecting materially poor people to the formal worship services of the local church(es)?

_____

_____

_____

2. How could the churches affiliated with your ministry be more accessible to materially poor believers and unbelievers? What could you do to help these churches improve in this area?

_____

_____

_____

CHAPTER SEVEN

RESISTING DEMONIC FORCES

What Adam and Israel failed to do—namely, drive the serpent from God's holy garden and extend his reign to the ends of the earth—the Last Adam and True Israel accomplishes once and for all. The serpent's head is crushed, and the powers of evil are disarmed (Rom. 16:20; Col. 2:14–15). Death and hell no longer have the last word.[1]

—MICHAEL HORTON, THEOLOGIAN, 2011

The point is clear: the first Christians lived in total dependence on the Holy Spirit. This is one of the most conspicuous differences between them and us. We rely on our organization, our education, our psychology, our finance . . . and so forth. We show little sign of any overdependence on the Holy Spirit. We despise faith and call it pietism. We regard spiritual realities as somewhat unreal, and are embarrassed to talk about them. They fit untidily into this secular age in which we live.[2]

—MICHAEL GREEN, THEOLOGIAN, 2002

K ing Jesus reigns over the entire cosmos—right now.

That simple statement is a declaration of war on Satan and his legions, who seek to exercise dominion in this fallen world. The forces of darkness and light clash in this war. Hence, living as citizens of God's kingdom is necessarily a battle against demonic forces.

As we saw in *Becoming Whole* chapter 7, demonic forces are particularly interested in keeping people in poverty, so—ironically— ending material poverty is nothing less than a spiritual battle. The last thing Satan wants is more restored priest-kings running around spreading the good news of Christ and His kingdom. From Satan's perspective, the fifty Kenyans with HIV/AIDS, Joy, Maurice, Cindy, and Bob are all defectors in an ongoing war. They were members of the kingdom of darkness, but now they are on the front lines of the advancement of the kingdom of light (Eph. 2:1–10; Col. 1:9–10). Satan loves poverty.

In this light, living in God's kingdom—including working to end poverty—is necessarily a battle against demonic forces:

> For our struggle is not against flesh and blood, but
> against the rulers, against the authorities, against the
> powers of this dark world and against the spiritual
> forces of evil in the heavenly realms. (Eph. 6:12)

Like all ministry, poverty alleviation is spiritual warfare, so we are told to put on the full armor of God to combat Satan and his schemes:

> Therefore put on the full armor of God, so that
> when the day of evil comes, you may be able to stand
> your ground, and after you have done everything, to
> stand. Stand firm then, with the belt of truth buckled
> around your waist, with the breastplate of righteous-
> ness in place, and with your feet fitted with the readi-
> ness that comes from the gospel of peace. In addition
> to all this, take up the shield of faith, with which
> you can extinguish all the flaming arrows of the evil
> one. Take the helmet of salvation and the sword of
> the Spirit, which is the word of God.
>
> And pray in the Spirit on all occasions with all
> kinds of prayers and requests. With this in mind, be
> alert and always keep on praying for all the Lord's
> people. (Eph. 6:13–18)

Note that spiritual warfare is fought not using the weapons of the world, but according to the ways of God. Truth holds us tight; convenient lies, misinformation, or manipulation do not. Gospel righteousness is meant to breed peace, not arrogant self-righteousness and distance. Faith rather than vengeance and retaliation is our defense, for faith takes us always to behold our gracious King. The gift of our salvation is a protection against thinking we can protect ourselves, and the Spirit powerfully works among us by His Word, bringing conviction and comfort in due course. How do we fight? By prayer. In humility. Seeking to be united as the people of God who aim to draw others into God's redeeming and renewing grace and love.

While demonic forces are to be taken seriously, we must remember that they are no match for King Jesus. Through His death on the cross, King Jesus has already defeated Satan and his legions, and He already reigns over every square inch of the universe (see Eph. 1:19–23; Col. 2:15). We do not have two equal powers who are battling, and there is no doubt who will be victorious. Christ alone is and will always be Lord. So, living into Christ's kingdom includes calling on His power to keep Satan at bay as we seek to push back the darkness.

Spirits

Resisting
demonic forces

Ministry Design Principle 20: All the ministry's stakeholders need to resist demonic forces by putting on the whole armor of God.

The influence of demonic forces in the world is deep and wide.[3] It is likely that Satan will attack the various ministry stakeholders in different ways, using methods that seem to work best depending on different cultural settings and personalities.

Sometimes demonic activity is overt, paralyzing materially poor people with fear that hinders their efforts to move out of poverty. For example, when my family and I lived in Uganda, we noticed that all the schools were closed. We learned that a cobbler in the town wasn't making much money repairing shoes, so he wanted to switch to a different line of business. Afraid of what the spirits might think of this move, he went to the local witch doctor seeking advice. The witch doctor told the cobbler that changing his line of business would upset the spirits, so the cobbler needed to sacrifice the heads of forty children to appease the spirits. As a result, the cobbler was going into schools to kidnap and behead students, causing the schools to close in order to keep the children safe.

Do not misunderstand: very few poor people across the entire Majority World would even consider behaving like this cobbler.[4] But this incident does illustrate the way that demons hold many people in the grip of fear, hampering their ability to move out of poverty. Hence, key features of poverty alleviation in the Majority World include explaining to materially poor people that Christ has defeated demonic forces and teaching them to put on the whole armor of God. In chapter 4, we saw an example of such teaching in the context of small business training (see Figure 4.3).

On the other hand, demonic forces also work covertly to ensure that people either think the spiritual realm does not exist (Western Naturalism) or that it is irrelevant to their material condition (Evangelical Gnosticism). And when they succeed in these endeavors, Western stakeholders will tend to put their trust in human know-how and material resources alone to accomplish their goals. Even when such approaches work at getting people out of material poverty, the demons can still quietly rejoice, for people who are achieving the American Dream are still far from becoming priest-kings who extend the reign and worship of Christ.[5] Hence, ministries that are trying to alleviate poverty in the West should explain to their stakeholders— including the materially poor people they are trying to help—that Satan is real and that he wants to trap them in a materialistic world-view. In chapter 4, we saw an example of how *Faith & Finances* tries to do this, teaching people that the goal is not to get rich but rather to advance Christ's kingdom.

Yes, the struggle is real, but it is not merely against flesh and blood.

Questions for Reflection:

1. How often do you pray for King Jesus to protect you from demonic forces?

_____

_____

_____

2. What does your answer to question 1 indicate about your understanding of how the cosmos works? Are there any ways in which you are functioning like an Evangelical Gnostic, who separates the spiritual and material realms?

_____

_____

_____

3. Reflect on the history of your poverty alleviation ministry. Can you list any times when Satan may have been attacking your work?

_____

_____

_____

4. List any specific actions that your ministry can commit to taking to better protect it from Satan's attacks.

_____

_____

_____

5. List any specific actions that your ministry can commit to taking to help materially poor people better protect themselves from Satan's attacks.

_____

_____

_____

FINAL WORD

East of Eden, we all are homeless beggars. Each one of us—whether we are materially rich or poor—is longing, like the Prodigal Son, to come home to a feast, a banquet at which our bodies and souls are fully satisfied and all our relationships are completely restored. The good news of the gospel of the kingdom is that, through Christ, homeless beggars can feast in God's dwelling place, the temple on His holy mountain, both *now and not yet*:[1]

> On this mountain the LORD Almighty will prepare
>   a feast of rich food for all peoples,
> a banquet of aged wine—
>   the best of meats and the finest of wines.
> On this mountain he will destroy
>   the shroud that enfolds all peoples,
> the sheet that covers all nations;
>   he will swallow up death forever.
> The Sovereign LORD will wipe away the tears
>   from all faces;
> he will remove his people's disgrace
>   from all the earth.
>   The LORD has spoken. (Isa. 25:6–8)

This is home, and there—and there alone—we are fully whole.

MINISTRY DESIGN PRINCIPLES

Community (Forming the kingdom community)

1. Christian poverty alleviation ministries must be "rooted in and lead back to" the local church.
2. Use supportive, gospel-centered groups as much as possible.

Story (Conquering false gods and erroneous stories of change)

3. All the ministry stakeholders should "pray without ceasing."
4. Narrate God's story of change throughout life.
5. Integrate God's story of change into technical training.
6. Use funding sources that permit God's story of change to be integrated into technical training.

Practices (Replacing destructive formative practices)

7. All the stakeholders should treat each other as members of a community that is jointly stewarding the King's gifts to advance His kingdom.
8. The ministry's marketing and communications should use images and messages that communicate God's story of change.
9. Learn from existing "best practices."
10. Use relief, rehabilitation, and development appropriately.
11. Start by focusing on assets, not needs.
12. Use participatory rather than blueprint approaches.

13. All interventions should be pro-work.
14. Encourage all stakeholders to give sacrificially.
15. Foster whole-person discipleship using adult education training techniques.

Systems (Addressing broken systems)
16. Address broken systems by navigating existing ones, creating alternatives, and/or reforming them altogether.

People (Addressing broken people)
17. Help people access physical and mental health care.
18. Verbally invite unbelievers to saving faith in Jesus Christ.
19. Invite materially poor people into the church's administration of the "ordinary means of grace."

Spirits (Resisting demonic forces)
20. All the ministry's stakeholders need to resist demonic forces by putting on the whole armor of God.

PROGRAM DESIGN: STORIES OF CHANGE AND LOGIC MODELS

What we have been calling a story of change in this book is commonly referred to as a "theory of change" in the social services sector, a statement of what the goal is and how that goal can be achieved.[1] A theory of change is often summarized by a "Logic Model," also called a Logical Framework or Log Frame, a tool that is increasingly being used to summarize the steps that an organization will take as it tries to achieve the desired goals.[2] A Logic Model articulates *what* the initiative will do, *how* it will do it, and *why* it matters.[3] Because a Logic Model articulates cause-and-effect claims about the various components of the program, it potentially allows for empirical verification of each of those claims.

As will be discussed below, there are some dangers in Logic Models, but one of their potential benefits is that they can help all the stakeholders—the financial resource partners, the ministry, and the materially poor people—get on the same page about the nature of the intervention and what is hoped to be accomplished.[4]

As pictured in Figure B.1, a Logic Model typically contains five components that outline the road map the organization will use to get from start to finish:

FIGURE B.1

The Logic Model

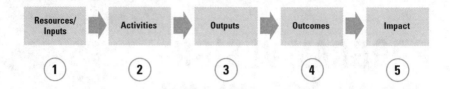

1. **Inputs:** the resources that will be used to do the work—such as community leadership, staff time, money, and malaria nets
2. **Activities:** the work that will be done with the resources—community training in proper use of malaria nets, for example
3. **Outputs:** the volume count of the amount of work that will get done—150 people trained and given malaria nets
4. **Outcomes:** the specific short-, medium-, and long-term changes in the individuals or communities that are anticipated—95% of villagers are sleeping under malaria nets
5. **Impact:** the ultimate benefits to be achieved—a reduction of malaria by 90%

Figure B.2 provides an example of a Logic Model for a secular HIV Testing and Counselling (HTC) Program.

As one would expect from a secular organization that has been influenced to some degree by Western Naturalism, the Logic Model in Figure B.2 has goals that are completely material: reducing sickness and death from HIV. And the way the organization seeks to achieve those goals are also reflective of naturalistic influences: use technology and technical know-how to conquer the material realm. Of course, Christians can agree that it is good to reduce sickness and death from HIV and that technology and education can help to achieve this goal.

But stop and think for a moment: What would the Logic Model in Figure B.2 look like if it were constructed from the perspective of a biblical story of change? Can you think of any differences? What would you would add, modify, or delete?

FIGURE B.2

Example of Logic Model for Secular HIV Testing and Counseling Program

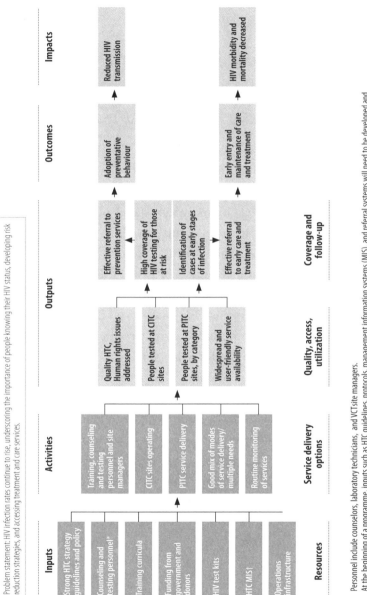

"Example of HTC Programme Logic Model," *Guide for Monitoring and Evaluating National HIV Testing and Counselling (HTC) Programmes*, field-test version (World Health Organization, 2011), 10, https://www.ncbi.nlm.nih.gov/books/NBK310781/.

From a biblical perspective, the ultimate *impact* for materially poor people—the item that belongs in the last box on the right in Figure B.2—should be:

The Goal of a Biblical Story of Change

*People experience human flourishing **when they serve as priest-kings**, using their mind, affections, will, and body to enjoy loving relationships with God, self, others, and the rest of creation.*

While it is impossible to create metrics that can fully measure such a holistic impact, a number of Christian organizations, including the Chalmers Center, are in various stages of developing metrics that at least get at some features of this goal.

We also believe that God's story of change has dramatic implications for the other four components of the Logic Model: *inputs, activities, outputs,* and *outcomes.* The Chalmers Center uses the Ministry Design Principles in this *Field Guide* as a checklist that informs and shapes all these components in our programs: *Faith & Finances* and *Work Life* in the US, and *Restore: Savings* and *Plan a Better Business* in the Majority World. Similarly, if we were designing an HIV testing and counseling program, these Ministry Design Principles would result in a Logic Model that would have some features that are the same as the ones in Figure B.2 (HIV test kits, for example), and some that would be different (such as connection to local church, use of supportive groups, biblically integrated curricula, different funding sources, prayer, and so on). Of course, Chalmers' Ministry Design Principles, Logic Models, and programs all are far from perfect, but this is how we are currently trying to improvise God's story of change in our work.

While Logic Models are potentially useful for carefully thinking through program design and for getting the stakeholders on the same page, they have potential problems as well.

First, who is creating the Logic Model? It is relatively easy for an experienced poverty alleviation organization to write down a Logic Model for a low-income community. And then if the organization has a good fundraising department, it won't be long before a new program is implemented. The problem with this approach is that it violates *Ministry Design Principle 13: Use participatory rather than blueprint approaches.*

Imagine how we would feel if a foreigner visited our neighborhood for a day, decided that we needed X, went out and raised money for X, and then came and imposed X on our neighborhood. We would feel a bit violated, wouldn't we? And maybe we don't even want X in our backyard. So, after the organizations builds X and leaves town, we have no intention of maintaining it. We didn't want X in the first place! Nonparticipatory approaches undermine "ownership," thereby reducing sustainability. And more deeply, they exacerbate the god-complex-marred-identity dynamic, resulting in disempowered image bearers. Real poverty alleviation is about *how* things get done, not just about *what* gets done.

Second, closely related to the previous issue, whose story of change is embedded in the Logic Model? If it's created by a secular organization, the Logic Model will likely reflect Western Naturalism. And if it's created by a Christian organization, the Logic Model will probably be under the influence of Evangelical Gnosticism. As we keep emphasizing, because we tend to *automatically* and *unconsciously* default to our culture, we end up imposing our culture's story of change, systems, and practices on materially poor people. And in the process, we ask them to be transformed into the image of whatever god(s) our culture is worshiping.

As secular development expert Robert Chambers so provocatively asked in the title of his famous book, *Whose Reality Counts?*, Chambers's answer to this question is revealed in his subtitle: *Putting the First Last.* Chambers powerfully argues that most poverty alleviation work is top-down, thereby allowing the educated and wealthy elites, those who are "first," to impose their view of reality—their story of change—on materially poor people. We concur with Chambers's assessment, and we agree that materially poor people need to have more voice and to "own" their process of change (Ministry Design Principles 8 and 13). That said, having materially poor people plan and direct their own lives doesn't solve the problem, for they too are *automatically* and *unconsciously* defaulting to their culture and its god(s).

So whose reality counts? Ultimately, only God's perspective counts. He reigns in His kingdom, so He is the only one who gets to define reality. The task for all the stakeholders (the financial resource partners, the ministry, and the materially poor participants) is to walk in light of His truth and in His power—to live in light of God's story of change. But while the Bible reveals much about God and His world, we must recognize that all Christians bring their own cultural biases into our interpretation of Scripture. Yes, there is absolute truth, but as finite and fallen creatures, we don't fully understand that truth. Moreover, unbelievers should be participants in our poverty alleviation ministries, for these ministries are part of our outreach to the world. And they will undoubtedly bring a very different perspective.

What should we do? Whose Logic Model, whose story of change, counts? The scope of this book does not permit an adequate discussion on how to handle these complex issues, but we are raising them to increase awareness and to bring light to the tensions that ministries must balance as they seek to be "in the world but not of it." Here are a few quick tips:

- Be humble. All of us are broken, and all of us are in process. None of us—believers or unbelievers—have truth all figured out.

- Recognize that materially poor people—not you—are called by God to be the primary stewards of their individual lives and communities. Ultimately, we have neither the authority nor the ability to impose God's story of change on materially poor people.

- Be quick to listen and slow to speak in your interactions with materially poor people, for you are not walking in their shoes, and their voices have generally not been heard. They have much to teach us if we will listen.

- Join with materially poor believers in praying for discernment about the best way to proceed. They too are being guided by God's Word and Spirit.

- Be participatory, but do not compromise with the world. For example, while a Christian ministry should be respectful to all people, it should not permit unbelievers to have the same status in directing the course of a ministry as the one true God and His revealed Word.

Third, Logic Models can perpetuate the lie of Western Naturalism that the world functions like a machine, so that poverty alleviation can be reduced to rational, controllable, linear processes.[5] As we have seen, the world just isn't like that. The five causes of poverty include complex human and social systems—not to mention demonic forces—that cannot be reduced to simple equations. Moreover, at the foundation of poverty alleviation are the supernatural actions of God Almighty, and He definitely cannot be controlled.

In light of the world's complexity and uncertainty, secular development experts are increasingly arguing that poverty alleviation needs to become less rigid and programmatic. What is needed, they say, is more of a learning process in which low-income individuals and communities develop the capacity to adapt to an ever-changing environment.[6] While there is some truth in this perspective, a biblical perspective recognizes that the stakeholders are not left to face this uncertainty alone, for the One who controls everything and for whom there is no uncertainty dwells among us and guides us by His Word and Spirit. In this light, in *Walking with the Poor*, Bryant Myers describes the use of Logic Models and other planning tools as follows:

> A truly Christian approach to designing a transformational development (poverty alleviation) program also needs to be open and attentive to what God has to say to us. Even more important, the [low-income] community needs to be invited to be open and

attentive to what God has to say to it. Together we need to be quiet and listen in the midst of all the information we have gathered and be open to God leading us to the information and conclusions that God deems most important.

We need to use the Bible, as the living Word of God, as a tool in our planning process. What might we hear from the Word that is relevant to determining what change really matters? What is God's best future for this community? Where is there evidence of God already being active?

Said another way, the process by which we work with the community is not just a problem-solving or appreciative exercise. It must be a spiritual exercise, an exercise in discernment. We need to integrate the methods of the spiritual disciplines into our development activities and use them as part of the development process. We must learn to be as spiritually discerning as we are professionally discerning.

We need to act and pray that our program design will, by God's grace, turn out to be part of God's ongoing work in the world. Our prayer needs to be that our program will become part of God's program, a program of transformation on which God has been working for all of human history. The unavoidable uncertainty of development work should drive us to continuing prayer as we realize that any transformational efforts in this fallen and chaotic world are an offering of our faith, hope, and love.[7]

Amen.

KEY THEMES OF
BECOMING WHOLE

Human beings are shaped by the story of change they embrace. Our story of change reflects our "metanarrative"—our understanding of God, humans, and how the world works. So, it is crucial that we immerse ourselves in the biblical metanarrative before we design our poverty alleviation ministries, for it is this overarching story that governs the real world in which we live.

THE NATURE OF GOD, THE WORLD, AND HUMAN BEINGS

From all eternity, the Father, Son, and Holy Spirit have existed in loving, intimate communion with one another. The love within the inner life of the Trinity overflows as God creates and cares for His world. Even after creation, He is "sustaining *all things* by his powerful word" (Heb. 1:3, emphasis added).

The fact that God, who is spirit, sustains His world means there is a material dimension and a spiritual dimension to the world. Humans, therefore, are not just physical creatures; rather, we are highly integrated bodies and souls. We may speak of three facets of the soul (or heart): the mind, affections, and will. Just as love is at the heart of the triune God, so love is at the heart of humans. And just as the creation flows from God's love, so too our actions flow from what we love.[1] Whatever our hearts love most determines our actions.

Reflecting our Creator and His designs, human beings are necessarily relational creatures, for the love in our hearts must be expressed toward someone or something.[2] Theologians underscore four fundamental human relationships emphasized in Scripture: relationships with God, self, others, and the rest of creation (see Gen. 1:26–28; Deut. 6:4–6).[3] Our relationship with God is central, foundational for the other three. God has designed these relationships to work in a certain way, and humans flourish only when we experience these relationships the way God intended. Since we are highly integrated mind-affections-will-body-relational creatures, whatever happens to us relationally affects our souls and bodies.

Some aspects of this mind-affections-will-body-relational creature can be illustrated by the image of a wheel (Figure C.1). The boundary of the human being is not the hub in the middle—the person's body and soul. Rather, the human being is the wheel as a whole, including both the person's body and soul (the hub) and their relationships (the spokes).

FIGURE C.1

Biblical View of the Human Being

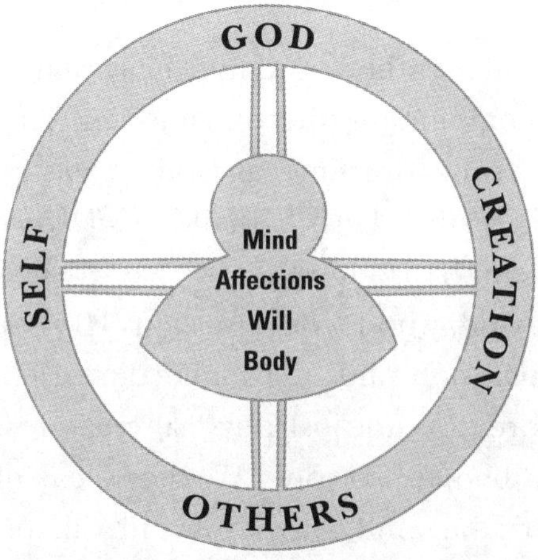

Adapted from Brian Fikkert and Russell Mask, *From Dependence to Dignity: How to Alleviate Poverty through Church-Centered Microfinance* (Grand Rapids: Zondervan, 2015), 83.

Each part of a wheel impacts the other parts. If one spoke is misaligned, pressure is placed on the other spokes and the hub. A broken relationship with creation—unemployment, for example—affects one's relationship to others and self. And just as a wheel's inner structure can be damaged by external forces, so can a human being's. Unemployment can be caused by an economic recession, the effects of which ripple through the entire person, impacting even the innermost being.

For more on this, see *Becoming Whole* chapter 1.

HOW DO HUMAN BEINGS AND CULTURES CHANGE?

Poverty alleviation is about change: helping low-income people move from their present condition to a better one. Some of what needs to change may be internal to the person, requiring modifications to their knowledge, attitudes, or behaviors. But some of the causes of poverty—systemic racism, for example—may be external to the person, requiring changes in cultural systems. Effective poverty alleviation, therefore, requires us to understand how both individuals and cultures change over time.

Humans are created to be image bearers: we mirror whatever god we are worshiping onto the rest of creation.[4] Worship in this context means more than singing a hymn. Whatever we love most is what we worship. And as we are transformed into the image of whatever god we worship, we then create culture in our own image.[5]

....

Worship and Poverty Alleviation

Human beings are transformed into the image of whatever god they worship, so at the core of poverty alleviation is worship of the one true God.

....

The Natural Process of Individual and Cultural Formation[6]

The god that a community is worshiping profoundly shapes its individual members through three channels:[7]

- Story of Change

- Formative Practices

- Environmental and Social Systems

These three channels shape each community member's individual personhood—their mind, affections, will, body, and relationships—to achieve the community's goals. Figure C.2 summarizes this process, highlighting how the elements of the community create a "formative feedback loop," a mutually reinforcing story of change, formative practices, systems, and personhoods that transform individuals and their cultures into the image of the god being worshiped.[8]

FIGURE C.2
The Natural Process of Individual and Cultural Formation

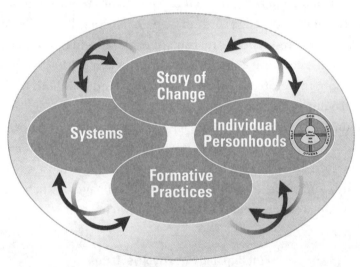

Adapted from Brian Fikkert & Michael Rhodes, "*Homo Economicus* Versus *Homo Imago Dei*,"
Journal of Markets & Morality, vol. 20, #1, 106.

The Gods People Worship

Because humans are transformed into the image of whatever god(s) they worship, effective poverty alleviation identifies the religious perspectives of *all* the stakeholders. Some scholars argue that there are three foundational religious perspectives in the world: *traditional religion, Western Naturalism,* and *historic Christianity,* with other religious perspectives being blends of these three (Figure C.3).[9]

FIGURE C.3
Three-Part Model of World Religious Perspectives

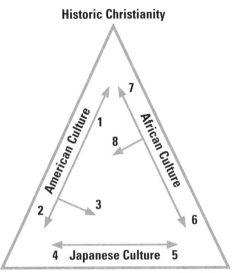

1) American Christians; 2) American Secularists; 3) New Agers in North America;
4) Western-influenced Japanese; 5) Shintoists; 6) African Traditional Religionists;
7) African Christians; 8) Secular influences radiating out of Christianity.

Adapted from Gailyn Van Rheenen, "Animism, Secularism, and Theism: Developing a Tripartite Model for Understanding World Cultures," *International Journal of Frontier Missions* 10(4), Oct. 1993, 171.

For more on how human beings and cultures change, see *Becoming Whole* chapter 2.

WHEN FALSE STORIES MAKE HELPING HURT

Most poverty alleviation efforts from the West have been shaped by Western Naturalism or Evangelical Gnosticism.[10] Consequently, these efforts typically involve an encounter between Western Naturalism or

Evangelical Gnosticism and the religious perspectives of materially poor people.

The False Story of Western Naturalism

Doubting God's existence or His relevance to the everyday working of the cosmos, Western Naturalism views all of reality as solely material. This material understanding extends to its view of humans. Instead of a mind-affections-will-body-relational creature, the human is viewed as a physical body that is highly individualistic, not needing relationships to flourish (Figure C.4). Purely material, this creature derives its happiness from consuming material things to gratify its sensual nature. And because this creature is largely non-relational, it selfishly pursues its own interests without regard for the effects it might have on its relationship with God, self, others, or the rest of creation.

FIGURE C.4

Western Naturalism's Deformation of the Human Being

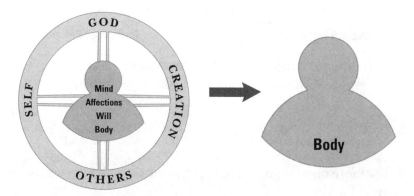

The false metanarrative of Western Naturalism results in the following story of change:

1. The goal is to consume more material things.
2. The way to achieve this goal is to increase people's income so they can buy more stuff.

Because many Westerners have internalized this story of change, they often *unconsciously* and *automatically* spread the virus of Western Naturalism to poor people in their poverty alleviation efforts, transforming them—at least partially—into the materialistic, individualistic, self-interested, consuming machine in Figure C.4. Western Civilization's materialistic perspective is seen in the two basic strategies it uses to alleviate material poverty:

- *Strategy #1: Handouts of Material Resources*

- *Strategy #2: Economic Empowerment*

For more, see *Becoming Whole* chapter 3.

The False Story of Evangelical Gnosticism

The Western church has often mixed Western Naturalism with historic Christianity (point 1 in Figure C.3), resulting in Evangelical Gnosticism. Gnosticism is a heresy that separates the spiritual realm, viewed as "good," from the material realm, seen as "bad." Evangelical Gnosticism confines God's reign to the spiritual dimension of reality and trusts the laws of nature to run the rest of the cosmos. Consequently, Western Christians worship God on Sunday but tend to live like Western Naturalists the rest of the week.

Separating the physical and spiritual realms impacts Evangelical Gnosticism's understanding of human beings (Figure C.5). Evangelical Gnosticism sees the body and soul as separable, with the soul being more important than the body. It also tends to reduce the soul to just the mind. Finally, it tends to view human beings as autonomous individuals rather than highly relational creatures.

FIGURE C.5
Evangelical Gnosticism's Deformation of the Human Being

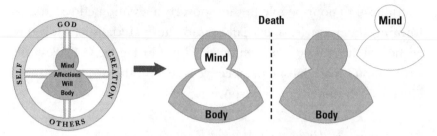

The goals of Evangelical Gnosticism's story of change, therefore, can be summarized as follows:

1. The primary goal is to get the soul to heaven for all eternity.
2. A secondary goal is to make the body happy in this life through self-centered, material consumption.

Because the spiritual and physical aspects of the human being are viewed as separate, Evangelical Gnosticism's goals for the body and poverty alleviation strategies are identical to Western Naturalism's, except that evangelism is added to save the soul:

- *Strategy #1: Handouts of Material Resources + Evangelism*
- *Strategy #2: Economic Empowerment + Evangelism*

For more, see *Becoming Whole* chapter 4.

GOD'S STORY OF CHANGE

The Two-Dimensional Cosmos of Western Christianity
Heavily influenced by Evangelical Gnosticism, Western Christians often live on a purely material plane, ignoring the spiritual dimension. Their focus has resulted in their world being reduced from three dimensions to two.

To comprehend God's story of change—for both materially poor people and ourselves—we need to realize the spiritual and the material realms are deeply integrated. We've been living in a two-dimensional world for so long that we can't even imagine a world with another dimension. It's not just that we haven't achieved the good life; it's that we don't even know what the good life is. We've unconsciously designed a story of change—for both ourselves and materially poor people—that makes sense in a two-dimensional world, but not in the real world in which we actually live. Thankfully, God has a different story for us to live into. To do so, we need to reimagine the biblical narrative.

For more, see *Becoming Whole* chapter 5.

Creation

The Garden of Eden functioned like a temple, where God and humans met.[11] Adam and Eve served as priests and kings in this garden-temple.[12] As priests, they were to protect the temple from corruption and lead others to worship God. As kings, they were to care for other people and creation by serving as God's vice-regents. As priest-kings, humans were to lovingly serve God, others, and the rest of creation, all of which necessitates a healthy view of "self." This leads to the following notion of human flourishing:

....

The Goal of a Biblical Story of Change

*People experience human flourishing **when they serve as priest-kings**, using their mind, affections, will, and body to enjoy loving relationships with God, self, others, and the rest of creation.*

....

As humans engaged in the task of developing God's creation in a sinless world, they would have made culture: art, business, sports, music, science, and more. Culture, therefore, is not inherently evil, but is the natural result of humans fulfilling their callings as priest-kings.

While God calls human beings to rule over His creation, He too remains intimately involved with it (see Col. 1:15–17). This means that while human beings have real *agency* (the calling, ability, and freedom) to develop the creation, we must do so within the bounds of God's providence. He upholds cultural systems, including governments, economies, schools, families, and farms; and He has every hair on our heads numbered. To capture this, Figure C.6 augments our natural process of individual and cultural formation to incorporate God's active presence in all creation:

FIGURE C.6

The Active Presence of God in Individual and Cultural Formation

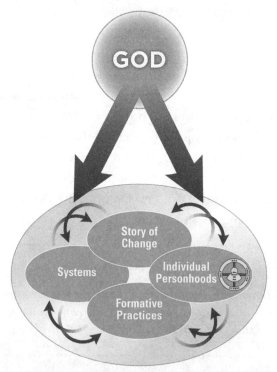

Adapted from Brian Fikkert & Michael Rhodes, "*Homo Economicus* Versus *Homo Imago Dei*," *Journal of Markets & Morality,* vol. 20, #1, 106.

For more, see *Becoming Whole* chapter 6.

The Fall

Western Christianity has tended to focus on the legal aspects of the fall: All people have sinned and are deserving of divine judgment. While true, the fall brings about so much more. Humans are hardwired for intimate relationship with God. So when Adam and Eve are cast out of the garden-temple, their entire personhoods are impacted (Figure C.7): their *relationship with self* is marred, their *relationship with others* is strained, and their *relationship with the rest of creation* is distorted (see Gen. 3:7–19; Rom 8:18–22). And the damage affects our minds, affections, wills, and bodies (see Ps. 32:1–5; 38; Rom. 1:18–32).[13] Yes, the fall gives us a legal problem, but it also gives us a human *being-ness* problem.

FIGURE C.7

The Impacts of the Fall on the Human Being

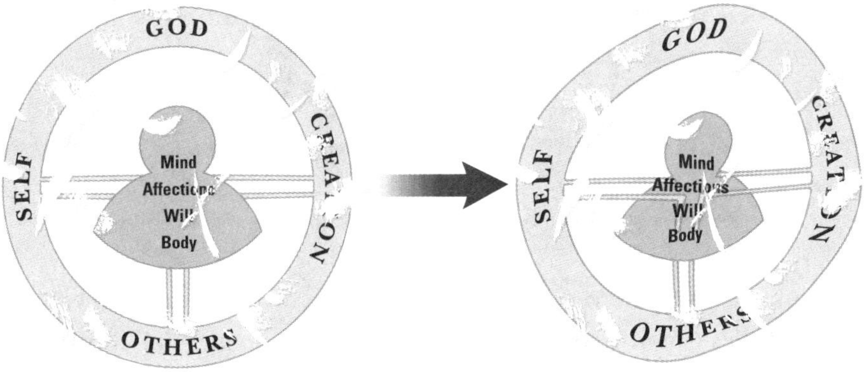

Adapted from Brian Fikkert and Russell Mask, *From Dependence to Dignity: How to Alleviate Poverty through Church-Centered Microfinance* (Grand Rapids: Zondervan, 2015), 91.

Moreover, broken people create broken cultures by adopting erroneous stories of change, engaging in destructive formative practices, and creating broken and oppressive systems. In addition to the mess created by human beings, demonic forces are unleashed to wreak even greater havoc in the world (see Figure C.8). We are talking about a cosmic problem when we are talking about the fall.

FIGURE C.8

The Model of Individual and Cultural Change in a Fallen World

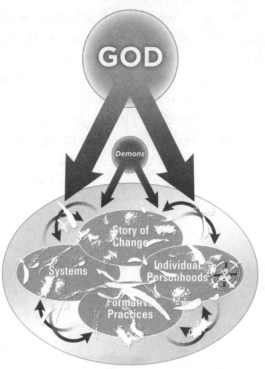

Adapted from Brian Fikkert and Michael Rhodes, "*Homo Economicus* Versus *Homo Imago Dei*,"
Journal of Markets and Morality 20, no. 1 (Spring 2017): 106.

All of this brokenness manifests itself in a myriad of ways in each of our lives. We all are *relationally poor*: none of us enjoy the four key relationships in the way God intended. And for some, this *relational poverty* leads to *material poverty*.

Redemption and Consummation

Western Christianity has also tended to focus mostly on the legal aspects of Christ's salvific work: Jesus died to forgive our sins. This is absolutely true and should never be diminished. Hallelujah! But Christ's life, death, and resurrection accomplish so much more.

Jesus is the promised King who is ushering in a kingdom, a new heaven and earth that will bring healing as far as the curse is found (see Luke 4:43). Although the kingdom will not be fully consummated until His second coming, Jesus has already conquered sin and death and is reigning over all things right now (see Eph. 1:18–23).

Moreover, Jesus' resurrection body is literally the beginning of the new creation. The kingdom is *not yet*, but it is definitely also *now!*

God's kingdom is much better news for poor people than Evangelical Gnosticism. Jesus doesn't just beam our souls up to heaven when we die. No, He is making all things new, overcoming all the causes of poverty:

1. False gods and erroneous stories of change
2. Destructive formative practices
3. Broken systems at both the community and macro levels
4. Broken people
5. Demonic forces

While we long for Jesus' kingdom to be fully consummated, these truths provide real hope for our whole being and all creation—both now and not yet. The key to human flourishing is for God to dwell with His people, just as He did in Eden. This is humanity's past, and it is redeemed humanity's future. In fact, the centerpiece of the conjoined new heaven and earth is a temple, a temple that harkens back to the Garden of Eden (see Rev. 22:1–2). The new creation is Eden restored![14]

But the restored Eden is not a return to the primitive state of Eden—the days before there was any culture. At the center of the new creation is a city, the New Jerusalem, that will include portions of this world's cultures (see Rev. 21:24). God will once again dwell with His people in a world without sin. And look how the Bible describes God's people in that city: "You have made them to be a *kingdom and priests* to serve our God, and they will *reign* on the earth" (Rev. 5:10; emphasis added). In the new creation, believers will be restored priest-kings, worshiping God and ruling with Him, just as humans were created to do in the very beginning! This is people restored to all that it means to be fully human!

For more, see *Becoming Whole* chapters 7 and 8.

The New Creation Dawns

Each of us is longing for Eden, longing to return to the dwelling place of God. Our entire being longs to worship, work, eat, play, sing, dance, and rest in the comfort and security of our heavenly Father's home.

Yes, poor people need malaria nets, clean water, and decent jobs to become whole, and we should work diligently to increase the availability of such things. But as important as these are, none of them is as foundational to sustainable poverty alleviation—as foundational to becoming fully whole—as being restored to God's dwelling place.

Of course, this presents quite a challenge! How can squatters in the slums of Manila, villagers in rural Uganda, public housing residents in Chicago—or any one of us, for that matter—be returned to God's dwelling place?

We can't get back to the temple on our own, so God sends Jesus Christ, who is *the* temple—the place where all the fullness of God *dwells* in bodily form (John 1:14; 2:18–22; Col. 2:9).

The New Testament describes believers as being *in Christ* and Christ as being *in* believers in a way analogous to the Father and Son being *in* each other.[15] *In Christ*, we are actually brought back into the temple! In fact, we are so in the temple that the church, the community of those who are *in Christ*, actually becomes the temple as well (1 Cor. 3:16–17; 1 Peter 2:4–5)!

Returning to God's dwelling place is so transformative that the Bible describes believers as a "new creation" (2 Cor. 5:17). In terms of our wheel analogy, being united to Christ and being filled with the Spirit is like restoring the spoke of our relationship to God. And this realigns every aspect of the mind-affections-will-body-relational creature, making us capable of becoming whole again (see Figure C.9).

Incompletely yet really, we already are what we will be in the new creation! Jesus is the firstfruits of the new creation (1 Cor. 15:20), and since we are *in Christ*, we have been spiritually resurrected with Him, making us firstfruits of the new creation as well (see Rom 8:23; James 1:18).

No, the kingdom is not yet fully consummated. Things are still

FIGURE C.9

The Restoration of the Human Being

Adapted from Brian Fikkert and Russell Mask, *From Dependence to Dignity: How to Alleviate Poverty through Church-Centered Microfinance* (Grand Rapids: Zondervan, 2015), 91.

very messy and complicated. We still wait for the final destruction of the indwelling sin with which we still wrestle, for Satan to be completely bound, for the resurrection of our bodies, and for the rest of creation to be liberated. Still, from the moment we become a Christian, we are "a new creation. The old has passed away; behold, the new has come" (2 Cor. 5:17 NIV). This is true human flourishing, and it is achieved through supernatural means:

· ·

The Way to Achieve the Goal of the Biblical Story of Change

Through the gift of the Son and Spirit, the triune God accomplishes our reconciliation to God, self, others, and the rest of creation.

· ·

For more, see *Becoming Whole* chapter 9.

LIVING INTO GOD'S STORY

God's story gives us a much bigger, better reason to get out of bed on Monday morning than the erroneous story of Evangelical Gnosticism, and it gives us much more power for doing so. As depicted in Figure C.10, we are re-created and called to embody the present and future reality of Christ's kingdom in the here and now of this broken world.

FIGURE C.10

A Community that Embodies God's Kingdom

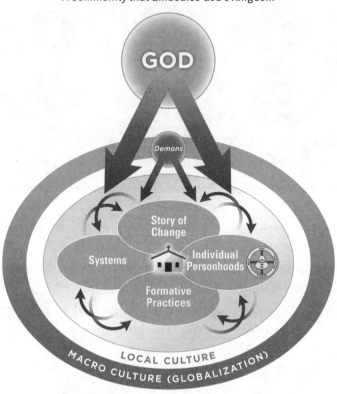

Adapted from Brian Fikkert and Michael Rhodes, "*Homo Economicus* Versus *Homo Imago Dei*,"
Journal of Markets and Morality 20, no.1 (Spring 2017), 106

The inner oval represents the emergence of the new creation within the existing culture, a community whose story of change, formative practices, systems, and members reflect the present reality of the kingdom of God. In the process, this community is necessarily engaged in poverty alleviation, for it is applying the power of Christ's death and resurrection to address the five causes of material poverty: false gods and erroneous stories of change, destructive formative practices, broken systems at both the community and macro levels, broken people, and demonic forces.

At the center of this community is the local church—the place where God dwells with His people in a special way. When the church assembles under its God-ordained authority to experience the ordinary means of grace, God has promised to be present by His Spirit.[16] Although these activities have no magical power in and of themselves, God has ordained these activities to be the normal means by which He calls people into saving faith and nurtures them in that faith, enabling them to serve Him more faithfully throughout the week.[17] In the process, individual brokenness is overcome. But reconciliation doesn't stop there: Christ uses His power to overcome all the other causes of relational and material poverty as well. One day, believers will be made completely whole.

In the meantime, each Sunday God's people gather for worship as restored priest-kings in His dwelling place. And then they seek to extend King Jesus' presence and reign throughout the earth from Monday through Saturday. In the process, all of creation gets a small foretaste of that great day when all will be made completely whole. Come, Lord Jesus, come!

NOTES

Preface

1. Phillis Wheatley, "Sabbath," in *Complete Writings*, ed. Vincent Carretta (New York: Penguin Books, 2001), 96.

Chapter 1: Improvising the Only True Story

1. N. T. Wright, *The New Testament and the People of God* (Minneapolis: Augsburg Fortress Press, 1992), 40.

2. Bryant L. Myers, *Walking with the Poor: Principles and Practices of Transformational Development*, revised and expanded ed. (Maryknoll, NY: Orbis Books, 2011), 55.

3. Crossroads Church and its ministry are real, but Absco is a fictional character, whose story is based on the actual experiences of millions of people in the Majority World.

4. See James K. A. Smith, *Desiring the Kingdom: Worship, Worldview, and Cultural Formation*, vol. 1, *Cultural Liturgies* (Grand Rapids: Baker Academic, 2009).

5. Gailyn Van Rheenen, "Animism, Secularism and Theism: Developing a Tripartite Model for Understanding World Cultures," *International Journal of Frontier Missions* 10, no. 4 (October 1993): 169–71. See also Darrow L. Miller with Stan Guthrie, *Discipling Nations: The Power of Truth to Transform Cultures* (Seattle: YWAM Publishers, 1998).

6. Carl F. Ellis Jr., *Free at Last? The Gospel in the African American Experience*, 2nd ed. (Downers Grove, IL: InterVarsity Press, 1996). Ellis says Western Civilization's inability to recognize the spiritual dimension of reality is similar to Flatland, an imaginary world in which two-dimensional shapes like circles and squares cannot even imagine a world of three dimensions, a world in which they would be spheres and cubes.

7. See Brian Fikkert and Kelly M. Kapic, *Becoming Whole: Why the Opposite of Poverty Isn't the American Dream* (Chicago: Moody Publishers, 2019), 249–50.

8. Adapted from Brian Fikkert, "God Has Chosen the Foolish and Despised Things," *Mandate*, newsletter of the Chalmers Center for Economic Development at Covenant College, vol. 1, no. 1, February 2007.

9. See Fikkert and Kapic, *Becoming Whole*, 251. For more about church-centered savings and credit associations, see Brian Fikkert and Russell Mask, *From Dependence to Dignity: How to Alleviate Poverty Through Church-Centered Microfinance* (Grand Rapids: Zondervan, 2015).

Chapter 2: Forming the Community of the Kingdom of God

1. Avery Dulles, *Models of the Church*, expanded ed. (New York: Image Books, 2002), 103.

2. Eugene H. Peterson, *Living the Resurrection: The Risen Christ in Everyday Life* (Colorado Springs: NavPress, 2006), 114.

3. Note that while the Bible indicates that the local church is called to care directly for the poor, this task is not given exclusively to the local church. In fact, the Bible indicates that the family, businesses, and even the state have roles to play in helping the poor. It takes wisdom in each situation to discern exactly which tasks the church should undertake directly with respect to the poor and which tasks should be left to other organizations, including parachurch ministries. For a fuller discussion of this issue, see Timothy J. Keller, *Center Church: Doing Balanced, Gospel-Centered Ministry in Your City* (Grand Rapids: Zondervan, 2012), 322–28.

4. Some of these principles were published earlier in Brian Fikkert and Russell Mask, *From Dependence to Dignity: How to Alleviate Poverty Through Church-Centered Microfinance* (Grand Rapids: Zondervan, 2015).

5. Bryant L. Myers, *Walking with the Poor: Principles and Practices of Transformational Development*, revised and expanded ed. (Maryknoll, NY: Orbis Books, 2011), 191.

6. Without question, there are varieties of "memorialist" accounts of the Lord's Supper, and debates about the particularities of the Eucharist are far beyond anything we can address here. But note, for example, that while the Protestant John Calvin rejected the Roman Catholic and Lutheran approaches to the Eucharist, which he thought were overly concerned about getting Christ somehow localized in the elements, he did not reject the importance of a particular divine presence through the Supper. But instead of Christ coming down in the elements, Calvin argued that by faith believers are elevated into the heavens. For more, see Keith A. Mathison, *Given for You: Reclaiming Calvin's Doctrine of the Lord's Supper* (Phillipsburg, NJ: P & R, 2002); J. Todd Billings, *Remembrance, Communion, and Hope: Rediscovering the Gospel at the Lord's Table* (Grand Rapids: Eerdmans, 2018).

7. Besides sources noted above, see also Sue A. Rozeboom, "Calvin's Doctrine of the Lord's Supper," in *Calvin's Theology and its Reception: Disputes, Developments, and New Possibilities*, J. Todd Billings and I. John Hesselink, eds. (Louisville: Westminster John Knox, 2012); Robert Letham, *The Lord's Supper: Eternal Word in Broken Bread* (Phillipsburg, NJ: P & R, 2001).

8. Leslie Newbigin, *The Gospel in a Pluralistic Society* (Grand Rapids: Wm. B. Eerdmans Publishing Company, 1989), 227.

9. See Brian Fikkert and Kelly M. Kapic, *Becoming Whole: Why the Opposite of Poverty Isn't the American Dream* (Chicago: Moody Publishers, 2019), chapter 6.

10. Interview with the author, 2006.

11. Brian Fikkert and Russell Mask, *From Dependence to Dignity: How to Alleviate Poverty Through Church-Centered Microfinance* (Grand Rapids: Zondervan, 2015), 261.

12. www.actscommunities.org and www.thinktank-inc.org.

13. Transcribed from video entitled "Joy Barnhill," https://actscommunities.org/resources, used by permission.

Chapter 3: Conquering False Gods and Erroneous Stories of Change

1. Martin Luther King Jr., "The False Gods We Worship," *The Papers of Martin Luther King, Jr., Volume VI: Advocate of the Social Gospel, September 1948–March 1963,* ed. Clayborne Carson, Susan Carson, Susan Englander, Troy Jackson, and Gerald L. Smith (Berkeley, CA: University of California Press, 2007), 134.

2. "Top 30 Greatest John Wesley Quotes—The Mind of a Missionary," February 6, 2016, https://smartandrelentless.com/top-30-john-wesley-quotes-the-mind-of-a-missionary.

3. All quotes in this story come from personal correspondence or recorded conversations with Maurice and Matt. They shared their stories as part of a testimonial for the Chalmers Center's *Faith & Finances* curriculum, which can be seen at https://vimeo.com/215516957.

4. New Generations, https://newgenerations.org/about-2-2.

5. Conversation with author, 2019.

6. Ibid.

7. See Brian Fikkert and Kelly M. Kapic, *Becoming Whole: Why the Opposite of Poverty Isn't the American Dream* (Chicago: Moody Publishers, 2019), chapter 6.

8. Michael Rhodes and Robby Holt with Brian Fikkert, *Practicing the King's Economy: Honoring Jesus in How We Work, Earn, Spend, Save, and Give* (Grand Rapids: Baker Books, 2018), 55.

9. See Fikkert and Kapic, *Becoming Whole,* chapter 3.

10. *Plan a Better Business Learning Conversations Facilitator's Guide* (Lookout Mountain, GA: Chalmers Center at Covenant College, 2009), 3. To learn more about this resource, visit www.chalmers.org/bhh.

11. J. Mark Bowers, *Faith & Finances* (Lookout Mountain, GA: Chalmers Center at Covenant College, 2012), 17–18.

12. Ibid., 120.

13. Ibid., 124.

14. Based on recall of the author, who was in the audience.

15. Bryant L. Myers, *Walking with the Poor: Principles and Practices of Transformational Development*, revised and expanded ed. (Maryknoll, NY: Orbis Books, 2011), 313.

Chapter 4: Replacing Destructive Formative Practices (Part 1)

1. Heart for Winter Haven, "A Tool for Transformation," Jobs for Life, May 1, 2018, https://www.jobsforlife.org/stories/detail/action,view/id,129#.XRvAd497mUk.

2. Advance Memphis, www.advancememphis.org.

3. Advance Memphis has enjoyed a fruitful relationship with Jobs for Life (www.jobsforlife.org) since fall 2005, a relationship that laid the foundation for Advance's jobs preparedness training for many years. Seeing the need for a curriculum that more fully addressed the context of multi-generational poverty, Advance and the Chalmers Center collaborated to create a new jobs training curriculum called *Work Life*, which Advance now uses and which Advance, Jobs for Life, and the Chalmers Center have been disseminating through various channels since 2015. For more information about this history, see http://advancememphis.org/wp-content/uploads/2015/08/Jobs-for-Life-to-Work-Life-Explanation-for-Web.pdf. For more information about *Work Life*, go to www.chalmers.org.

4. Although we can take no credit for their incredible success, the Chalmers Center has enjoyed a relationship with Advance Memphis since the inception of both organizations in 1999. Advance has collaborated with the Chalmers Center in creating both *Faith & Finances* and *Work Life* and has also hosted numerous interns from the Department of Economics and Community Development at Covenant College (www.covenant.edu), which is joined at the hip with the Chalmers Center.

5. Advance Memphis' entrepreneurship program is based on LAUNCH Chattanooga (www.launchchattanooga.org) and the Co.Starters course (www.costarters.co).

6. https://www.jobsforlife.org.

7. Cindy Chapple, "My Life Has Radically Changed," November 19, 2010, reprinted by permission of Advance Memphis, https://advancememphis.org/my-life-has-radically-changed.

8. See Brian Fikkert and Kelly M. Kapic, *Becoming Whole: Why the Opposite of Poverty Isn't the American Dream* (Chicago: Moody Publishers, 2019), chapter 2.

9. See ibid., chapter 1.

10. For more on this dynamic, see Kelly M. Kapic, *A Little Book for New Theologians:*

Why and How to Study Theology (Downers Grove, IL: IVP Academic, 2012), 21–29, 41–48.

11. See Fikkert and Kapic, *Becoming Whole*, chapter 2.

12. See ibid., chapter 4.

13. See, for example, Muhammad Yunus, *Creating a World Without Poverty: Social Business and the Future of Capitalism* (New York: Public Affairs, 2008); David Bornstein, *How to Change the World: Social Entrepreneurs and the Power of New Ideas* (Oxford, UK: Oxford University Press, 2007).

14. See Fikkert and Kapic, *Becoming Whole*, chapter 10.

Chapter 5: Replacing Destructive Formative Practices (Part 2)

1. "Resources in Action: Donald Jenkins," Release Your Raise, releaseyourraise .wordpress.com/2014/11/21/resources-in-action-donald-jenkins/.

2. Tish Harrison Warren, *Liturgy of the Ordinary: Sacred Practices in Everyday Life* (Downers Grove, IL: InterVarsity Press, 2016), 34.

3. Ministry Design Principles 10–12 are covered in greater depth in chapters 4–6 of Steve Corbett and Brian Fikkert, *When Helping Hurts: How to Alleviate Poverty without Hurting the Poor . . . and Yourself*, 2nd ed. (Chicago: Moody Publishers, 2012).

4. This is a modification of a definition found in Roland Bunch, *Two Ears of Corn: A Guide to People-Centered Agricultural Improvement* (Oklahoma City, OK: World Neighbors, 1982).

5. Alvin Mbola, "Bad Relief Undermines Worship in Kibera," *Mandate*, Chalmers Center for Economic Development, 2007, no. 3.

6. A host of resources for pursuing asset-based community development in the US can be found at the ABCD Institute at Northwestern University: https:// community-wealth.org/content/asset-based-community-development-institute- abcd-northwestern-university. For tools to use with an asset-based approach with individuals in the US, see Steve Corbett and Brian Fikkert with Katie Casselberry, *Helping Without Hurting in Church Benevolence: A Practical Guide to Walking with Low-Income People* (Chicago: Moody Publishers, 2015). Consider also the ACTS process of Think-Tank: https://www.thinktank-inc.org/services. When working in the Majority World, an asset-based approach to community development is called "participatory learning and action." The "Church and Community Mobilization" resources of Tearfund UK are an excellent place to start: https://learn.tearfund .org/en/themes/church/church_and_community_mobilisation.

7. "Flip the List," Jobs for Life, https://www.jobsforlife.org/FliptheList.

8. For more on the theme of connecting the cross, imitating Christ, and sacrificial giving, see Kelly M. Kapic with Justin Borger, *The God Who Gives: How the Trinity Shapes the Christian Story* (Grand Rapids: Zondervan, 2018), 189–210.

9. See *Becoming Whole*, chapter 6.

10. James E. Zull, *From Brain to Mind: Using Neuroscience to Guide Change in Education* (Sterling, VA: Stylus Publishing, 2011). See also the learning theory in D. A. Kolb, *Experiential Learning: Experience as the Source of Learning and Development* (Englewood Cliffs, NJ: Prentice-Hall, 1984).

11. Malcolm S. Knowles, Elwood F. Holton III, and Richard A. Swanson, *The Adult Learner: The Definitive Classic in Adult Education and Human Resource Development* (Oxford, UK: Elsevier, 2011).

12. Jane Vella, *On Teaching and Learning: Putting the Principles and Practices of Dialogue Education into Action* (San Francisco: Jossey-Bass, 2008); Jane Vella, *Learning to Listen, Learning to Teach: The Power of Dialogue in Educating Adults* (San Francisco: Jossey-Bass, 2002). Global Learning Partners provides a host of additional training and tools to equip trainers in all aspects of dialogue education, and readers are encouraged to visit their website for more information: www.globallearningpartners.com.

13. Darlene M. Goetzman, *Dialogue Education Step by Step: A Guide for Designing Exceptional Learning Events* (Montpelier, VT: Global Learning Partners, 2012).

Chapter 6: Addressing Broken Systems and Broken People

1. Michael O. Emerson and Christian Smith, *Divided by Faith: Evangelical Religion and the Problem of Faith in America* (Oxford, UK: Oxford University Press, 2001), 170.

2. Interview with staff of the Chalmers Center, 2012.

3. See Brian Fikkert and Kelly M. Kapic, *Becoming Whole: Why the Opposite of Poverty Isn't the American Dream* (Chicago: Moody Publishers, 2019), chapter 7.

4. Emerson and Smith, *Divided by Faith*, 76–77.

5. Ibid., 41, 76–77.

6. The Chalmers Center's online course *Are You a Good Neighbor?* is an excellent tool to help you take practical steps to this kind of relationship development: www.areyouagoodneighbor.org.

7. For more information about the potential of various forms of microfinance to address broken financial systems, see Brian Fikkert and Russell Mask, *From Dependence to Dignity: How to Alleviate Poverty Through Church-Centered Microfinance* (Grand Rapids: Zondervan, 2015).

8. Steve Corbett and Brian Fikkert, *When Helping Hurts: How to Alleviate Poverty without Hurting the Poor . . . and Yourself*, 2nd ed. (Chicago: Moody Publishers, 2012), 234–36, 243, 251–57.

9. See Fikkert and Kapic, *Becoming Whole*, chapter 7.

10. Anirudh Krishna, *One Illness Away: Why People Become Poor and How They Escape Poverty* (Oxford, UK: Oxford University Press, 2010), 71.

11. Ibid., 73.

12. Corbett and Fikkert, *When Helping Hurts*, 64–66.

13. Craig Brian Larson, "Communion When Seekers Are Present," *CT Pastors*, Spring 1995, https://www.christianitytoday.com/pastors/1995/spring/5l2071 .html.

Chapter 7: Resisting Demonic Forces

1. Michael Horton, *Pilgrim Theology* (Grand Rapids: Zondervan, 2011), 206.

2. Michael Green, *Thirty Years That Changed the World: The Book of Acts for Today*, 2nd ed. (Grand Rapids: Eerdmans, 2002), 284.

3. See Brian Fikkert and Kelly M. Kapic, *Becoming Whole: Why the Opposite of Poverty Isn't the American Dream* (Chicago: Moody Publishers, 2019), chapter 7.

4. For examples of the continuing reality of witch doctors, see Bob Goff, *Everybody Always: Becoming Love in a World Filled with Setbacks and Difficult People* (Nashville, TN: Thomas Nelson, 2018), 183–85, 215–17.

5. C. S. Lewis consistently makes a version of this point in *The Screwtape Letters* (New York: HarperCollins Publishers, 2001), 31: "Our policy, for the moment, is to conceal ourselves. . . . When [humans] believe in us, we cannot make them materialists and skeptics. . . . I do not think you will have much difficulty in keeping [humans] in the dark. The fact that 'devils' are predominantly comic figures in the modern imagination will help you. If any faint suspicion of your existence begins to arise in his mind, suggest to him a picture of something in red tights and persuade him that since he cannot believe in that . . . he therefore cannot believe in you."

Final Word

1. Timothy Keller, *The Prodigal God: Recovering the Heart of the Christian Faith* (New York: Dutton, 2008).

Appendix B: Program Design: Stories of Change and Logic Models

1. See the Center for Theory of Change: www.theoryofchange.org.

2. A helpful resource is *Logic Model Development Guide: Using Logic Models to Bring Together Planning, Evaluation, and Action* (Battle Creek, MI: W.K. Kellogg Foundation, 2004), available at https://www.wkkf.org/resource-directory/resource/2006/02/wk-kellogg-foundation-logic-model-development-guide.

3. Peter Frumkin, "Social Impact Strategy: Tools for Entrepreneurs and Innovators," online course from University of Pennsylvania available at www .socialimpactstrategy.org.

4. For helpful discussions of some of these pros and cons, see Bryant L. Myers, *Walking with the Poor: Principles and Practices of Transformational Development*, revised and expanded ed. (Maryknoll, NY: Orbis Books, 2011), 239–48; Paul

Brest, "The Power of Theories of Change," *Stanford Social Innovation Review* (Spring 2010): 47–51.

5. Myers, *Walking with the Poor*, 243–47.

6. Ibid.

7. Ibid., 247–48.

Appendix C: Key Themes of *Becoming Whole*

1. James K. A. Smith, *Desiring the Kingdom: Worship, Worldview, and Cultural Formation*, Cultural Liturgies, vol. 1 (Grand Rapids: Baker Academic, 2009), 51–52.

2. This relational dynamic as central to human persons is widely recognized beyond merely drawing from Scripture. See, for example, how David Brooks explores this idea in terms of psychology, relationality, etc., in *The Social Animal: Hidden Sources of Love, Character, and Achievement* (New York: Random House, 2011).

3. For example, see Anthony A. Hoekema, *Created in God's Image* (Grand Rapids: William B. Eerdmans Publishing Company, 1986), 75–111.

4. Richard Lints, *Identity and Idolatry: The Image of God and Its Inversion* (Downers Grove, IL: IVP Academic, 2015), 18–19. See also J. Richard Middleton, "The Liberating Image? Interpreting the Imago Dei in Context," *Christian Scholars Review* 24, no. 1 (1994): 8–25.

5. Bob Goudzwaard, *Aid for the Overdeveloped West* (Toronto, ON: Wedge Publishing Foundation, 1975), 14–15.

6. This section is adapted from Fikkert and Rhodes, "*Homo Economicus* Versus *Homo Imago Dei*," in *Journal of Markets and Morality* 20, no. 1 (Spring 2017): 105–106. I (Brian) am extremely grateful to Michael Rhodes for increasing my understanding of this process.

7. See Alasdair C. MacIntyre, *After Virtue: A Study in Moral Story*, 3rd ed. (Notre Dame, IN: University of Notre Dame Press, 1981).

8. Fikkert and Rhodes, "*Homo Economicus*," 104.

9. Van Rheenen, *Animism, Secularism and Theism*, 169–71. See also Miller, *Discipling Nations*.

10. Miller, *Discipling Nations*. See also Thabiti Anyabwile, "Evangelical Gnosticism," The Gospel Coalition, April 11, 2018, https://www.thegospelcoalition.org/blogs/thabiti-anyabwile/evangelical-gnosticism/; Abigail Rine Favale, "Evangelical Gnosticism," *First Things*, May 2018, https://www.firstthings.com/article/2018/05/evangelical-gnosticism.

11. See Gordon J. Wenham, *Genesis 1-15*, Word Biblical Commentaries (Waco, TX: Word Books, 1987), 61–62, 86; G. J. Wenham, "Sanctuary Symbolism in the Garden of Eden Story," *Proceedings of the World Congress of Jewish Studies* 9 (1986),

19–25. G. K. Beale has been one of the leaders in highlighting this theme. See *The Temple and the Church's Mission* (Downers Grove, IL: Apollos IVP, 2004), 66–80; idem, *New Testament Biblical Theology: The Unfolding of the Old Testament in the New* (Grand Rapids: Baker Academic, 2011), 617–22. Ancient Jewish literature sometimes struggled with this idea of the garden on earth, since this is where God abides, and therefore sometimes imagined it might actually be in heaven, see James L. Kugel, *The Bible as It Was* (Cambridge, UK: Harvard University Press, 1997), 80–82.

12. T. Desmond Alexander, *From Eden to New Jerusalem* (Grand Rapids: Kregel Publications, 2016); G. K. Beale and Mitchell Kim, *God Dwells Among Us: Expanding Eden to the Ends of the Earth* (Downers Grove, IL: InterVarsity Press, 2014); J. Richard Middleton, *A New Heaven and a New Earth: Reclaiming Biblical Eschatology* (Grand Rapids: Baker Academic, 2014); T. Desmond Alexander, *From Paradise to the Promised Land* (Grand Rapids: Baker Academic, 2012); N. T. Wright, *After You Believe: Why Christian Character Matters* (New York: HarperOne, 2012); Beale, *The Temple and the Church's Mission.*

13. Fikkert and Mask, *From Dependence to Dignity*, 90–91; Corbett and Fikkert, *When Helping Hurts*, 58.

14. Beale and Kim, *God Dwells Among Us*, 21.

15. For those new to this topic, see the very helpful article by Justin Taylor, "Union with Christ: A Crash Course," The Gospel Coalition, February 9, 2011, thegospelcoalition.org/blogs/justintaylor/2011/02/09/union-with-christ-a-crash-course. Taylor rightly points to the following passages as formative in shaping this doctrine: John 6:56; 15:4–7; Rom. 8:10; 1 Cor. 15:22; 2 Cor. 12:2; 13:5; Gal. 2:20; 3:28; Eph. 1:4; 2:10; 3:17; Phil. 3:9; Col. 1:27; 1 Thess. 4:16; 1 John 4:13.

16. See Westminster Larger Catechism (Qs. 154–188) and Shorter Catechism (Qs. 88–99) for classic brief statements on the "outward" (sometimes called "ordinary" or "normal") means of grace. For an overview of a Protestant (Reformed) view of the means of grace, with special attention to Word and sacrament, see Michael Horton, *The Christian Faith: A Systematic Theology for Pilgrims On the Way* (Grand Rapids: Zondervan, 2011), 751–87.

17. Some ecclesiastical traditions would add several other items to the list, and some would subtract "prayer." For an accessible and helpful introduction to this topic, see Luke Stamps, "Especially Preaching: The Ordinary Means of Grace and Christian Spirituality," The Gospel Coalition, February 10, 2011, http://thegospelcoalition.org/article/especially-preaching-the-ordinary-means-of-grace-and-christian-spirituality.

We tend to focus on spiritual needs without addresses other facets.

The World Happiness Report — Harvard
loneliness is rampant, like 15 cigarettes/d[a]

Happiness around the world Carol Graham !

Broken people create broken systems

The
Chalmers
Center

Take the next step toward a biblical approach to poverty.

Whether you're just starting out or have walked alongside people who are poor for years, Chalmers can help you discover better ways to love the poor.

 chalmers.org

WESTERN CIVILIZATION IS WEALTHIER, BUT IT ISN'T HAPPIER.

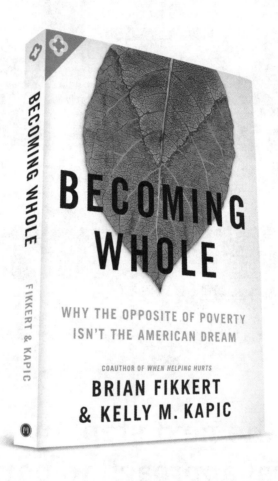

BECOMING WHOLE

WHY THE OPPOSITE OF POVERTY ISN'T THE AMERICAN DREAM

COAUTHOR OF *WHEN HELPING HURTS*

BRIAN FIKKERT & KELLY M. KAPIC

MOODY Publishers®

From the Word to Life®

Brian Fikkert and Kelly M. Kapic uncover the failures of current poverty alleviation strategies and reveal that the source of the problem lies in our beliefs. They demonstrate that community transformation begins with changed hearts and that God's design for change is the only one that works.

978-0-8024-0158-8 | also available as an eBook

HOW TO ALLEVIATE POVERTY
WITHOUT HURTING THE POOR . . .
AND YOURSELF

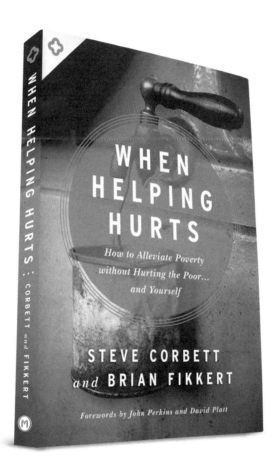

When Helping Hurts is a practical tool to help your ministry or team make a real long-term difference in the plight of the poor or suffering. This book provides foundational concepts, clearly articulated general principles, and relevant applications that keep you from strategies that do more harm than good.

978-0-8024-0998-0 | also available as an eBook